FROM ARREST TO RELEASE

The Inside/Outside Survival Guide

Before becoming a writer, Shirley Cooklin was a successful stage, television and radio actress. She has written plays for radio, and now writes full-time for television, including for series such as 'EastEnders' and 'The Bill'.

For many years she visited prisons as a voluntary associate (VA) of the Inner London Probation and After-Care Service, and spoke out about penal issues. This experience led her to write *Knockback* with Peter Adams, an account of a VA's relationship with a 'lifer' which was subsequently adapted for BBC Television.

In 1984 she founded the Ben Bryant Trust in memory of her son, who died with 18 others when the barque Marques sank during that year's Tall Ships Race. The charity provides dinghy sailing tuition for deprived inner-city children as an adventurous alternative to anti-social activities.

Shirley Cooklin is currently campaigning, with the bereaved from other Department of Transport disasters, for public inquiries to become independent of government, and for legal aid to become a right for bereaved parties.

FROM ARREST TO RELEASE

The Inside/Outside Survival Guide

Shirley Cooklin

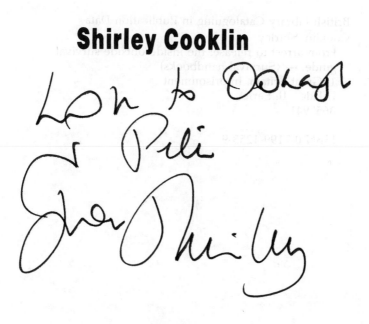

Bedford Square Press

Published by
BEDFORD SQUARE PRESS of the
National Council for Voluntary Organisations
26 Bedford Square, London WC1B 3HU

First published 1989
© Shirley Cooklin, 1989

Typeset by Book Ens, Saffron Walden, Essex

Printed and bound in England by
The Camelot Press Ltd, Southampton

British Library Cataloguing in Publication Data
Cooklin, Shirley
    From arrest to release: the inside/outside survival
    guide. — (Survival handbooks)
    1. Great Britain. Imprisonment
    I. Title   II. Series
    365'.941

    ISBN 0-7199-1253-9

Contents

Foreword

From Arrest to Release is an important and timely book. At
present the UK possesses the dubious honour of sending more
people to prison than any other major European country
including Turkey. In England and Wales alone there are about
50,000 people in custody, and the Prison Department is
preparing itself for a prison population of between 63,000 and
69,000 by the year 1996. More people than ever before will
suffer either directly or indirectly from imprisonment.

This rise is not inevitable. Imprisonment is an expensive
option, as Shirley Cooklin explains, both in terms of cost to the
public purse and in the misery it inflicts on innocent victims. Its
overuse is a matter of choice, the present choice being to enable
courts to send people to prison instead of using the many
constructive alternatives. As a result we have the unfortunate
combination of the highest prison population and the most
restricted opportunities for contact between prisoners and their
visitors in almost all of Western Europe.

On her first ever visit to a prison the author was struck by
the existence of two waiting rooms, one for lawyers visiting
their clients inside, the other for the friends and relatives of
prisoners. This is a potent symbol of the degree of
discrimination suffered by prisoners' visitors. All too often they
have to learn to understand and cope with the strange and alien
workings of the penal system in inadequate, sometimes squalid
waiting rooms and visiting areas with no proper information to
guide them.

A major strength of this book is its extensive and wide–
ranging nature, covering as it does the whole penal process
from arrest, the courts and prison through to release and after.
It is also speaks on a personal and accessible level to people

who are faced with the problem of dealing with the penal system, and should do much to increase their confidence, reduce their fear of the unknown and inform them of their rights.

Vivien Stern
Director, National Association for the Care and Resettlement of Offenders (NACRO)

Preface

It may seem strange to some that, as a playwright, a writer of fiction, I should have elected to write a book of practical information. The reasons date back to 1971 when I became a VA (voluntary associate) and embarked on 10 years of voluntary prison visiting in my spare time. Eventually I visited prisons all over England and took on dozens of cases, but at the time I began I knew very little, either about the criminal justice system or why it was that some people went to prison and others did not. Neither did I have a very clear idea of why I was doing this kind of voluntary work.

My very first visit, to Wandsworth prison in South London, had a profound effect on me. The young man I went to see was what social workers call 'a recidivist' (or, less politely sometimes, 'an inadequate'). Waiting inside the gate to go in I was struck at once by the fact that solicitors had a separate room to wait in. That was my first intimation that prisoners' visitors are seen as 'them' rather than 'us'; as part of the system and only a degree better than those they are going in to see. I also noticed that solicitors (and others of the professional classes) were notably absent from the crowded waiting room. When at last I had progressed beyond the gate, to the ante-room of the visiting room, I saw that there was no handle on the door and realised I was, for the first time ever to my knowledge, locked in. This was not a pleasant sensation. The fourth thing that struck me was that everyone else appeared at their ease: visiting a prison was to them a fact of life and not something shocking or strange as it was to me, a newcomer to the system. They, it seemed, had accepted that they were 'them'.

When I finally met my chap, a pale young man in prison–issue striped denim, I was startled to see he had naked starvation written on his face; not hunger for food but for human contact. He reminded me of someone in a desert, to whom a drink of water might represent life itself. I soon saw that in this case *I* was the glass of water and finally began to understand why I had become a VA and why ordinary people like me needed to play a part in the criminal justice system.

It is my 10 years' experience as a VA that qualifies me to write this book, and my belief that we should *all* know something of what is being done in our name – in the name of 'society' – that is my reason for writing it. Prison is an expensive option, both in terms of cost to the public purse and in the misery it inflicts upon innocent victims: the partners and families of prisoners; the children whose mothers have been taken from them (often for trivial and non–violent first offences) and who are put into care.

From attending NACRO conferences in the 1970s I know that successive Home Secretaries have paid lip service to the fact that two–thirds of the prison population do not represent a danger to the community and could be dealt with other than by being given a custodial sentence. There was talk, in 1971 when I was a novice VA, of the need for more hostel options and more probation officers; of the need for keeping non–violent offenders out of prison and gearing the custodial system to deal exclusively (and more humanely) with those who *must* be locked away for the protection of the public. From the media I know that this is still being said and that nothing has changed. Instead we continue to build more prisons and the system we still employ continues to become even more expensive. We lock up around 50,000 people at any one time, of whom one in five has not been convicted of any offence, a quarter are teenagers and at least two–thirds are non–violent. Even though they may be anti–social, this should be weighed against the fact that it costs a staggering £14,775 to keep one person in prison for a year.

Soon after I became a VA, I began to form the view that I might be more productively employed in doing something to prevent people going into the system in the first place rather than (as a criminologist friend once accused me) by spending time 'pacifying prisoners'. It seemed to me then, and it seems to me now, that the answer must lie in aiming resources at prevention rather than cure and looking at ways of preventing the schoolchildren of today becoming the offenders (and the prison fodder) of tomorrow.

The problem of how to do this remains a tough one. But I remain convinced that the first step is to identify the problem and the second to try to find ways of solving it. As a society we tend to be apathetic about what is being done in our name by the government and to think it has nothing to do with us; but it does, and the health and stability of future generations depends on it. At present all we are doing is ensuring a cycle of deprivation. The largest section of the criminal population of this country is of males aged 15. They were not criminalised overnight, and no one will convince me that some 9–year–olds who have gone on to become 10–year–old villains (10 is the age of criminal responsibility) might not have been 'caught' early and steered in a more productive and less anti–social direction.

It is my hope that this book will be of use to those both 'inside' and 'outside' who have to deal with the prison system and the law; that it will be helpful to those who assist prisoners or their families, the advice agencies, the self–help and support groups, probation officers, VAs, solicitors and others; that it will be a useful source of information for students, writers, programme makers and all who need information on this subject in a readily accessible form. But I admit also to a hope that it may act as a source of enlightenment to those who, in the ordinary way, are unlikely to ever acquire first–hand knowledge of the system. While not everyone has the time, the will or the wish to become a VA and find out for themselves what goes on at grass–roots level, we could all, if we were better informed, feel that we had a voice and the right to express an opinion on whether resources are being spent to the best effect.

This book, therefore, has three voices and, it is hoped, three types of reader. First, it is for anyone involved in the system at first hand, whether they simply want to help a friend appearing in court or to know about their rights in prison. Second, it is for the visitors of prisoners. I hope that I shall not cause offence by having written as if all prisoners were men and all visitors women. Although everything that is said applies to either sex, the great majority of prisoners are men and the great majority of visitors are the partners, wives and families of men doing time. By the same token, prison officers are generally referred to by the male pronoun.

The information for women prisoners is the same as it is for men, but additional information is included about womens' special problems in the criminal justice system. There can be little doubt that women prisoners *are* disadvantaged or that they suffer harsher treatment and are imprisoned more often for non–violent first offences. Although fewer women than men receive custodial sentences, overall the female percentage of the prison population is rising substantially faster. Most civilised people believe that to lock up a pregnant woman (unless she is patently dangerous) is nothing short of barbaric, and I hope that the third reader – 'society' – may at least consider the plight of such women and of the children who become the innocent victims of this recurring cycle of deprivation.

Black people are also disadvantaged in the criminal justice system; statistical evidence shows they are more likely to be stopped on the streets, less likely to be cautioned, more likely to be taken into custody (in spite of having fewer previous convictions) and more likely to end up in closed conditions. Although black people make up just over 4 per cent of the population in the UK, the percentage of black prisoners has risen from 12.5 per cent in 1985 to 14 per cent in 1987. Less than 2 per cent of magistrates and probation officers and fewer than 1 per cent of prison staff are black. Clearly there is room for change.

I have attempted in this book to avoid expressing my opinion and to report facts faithfully and simply. This edition covers England and Wales only. While every attempt has been made to ensure that the information is up to date at the time of going to press (May 1989), changes occur rapidly in the penal and legal systems. You are therefore always advised to seek professional legal advice on any criminal matter.

Every single one of us, like it or not, is affected by what goes on in our criminal justice system. At present we spend ever-increasing sums on teaching young people how to become bigger and better criminals by putting them in prison. Instead, we should be trying to find ways to solve the problem of converting them into responsible citizens. I hope that the information on these pages may help to shed some light on this dark area of the world – that same world in which, finally, lies the future of *all* our children.

Acknowledgements

My grateful thanks to all who made this book possible: especially to Elisabeth Rawlinson (Prisoners' Wives Service) and Pauline Hoare (Prisoners' Wives and Families) who helped me to see what the book should contain, and gave help and advice so freely; to Stephen Shaw (director of the Prison Reform Trust) for permission to reproduce copyright material from *Visiting Prisons*, allowing me to use material from the 'Prisoners' Information Pack' and generously giving his time to check the manuscript; to Judy Wilson (Women in Prison) for opening my eyes to the disadvantages suffered by women in the criminal justice system; to NACRO for permission to use the leaflet 'Children', produced by the Prisons Link Unit, and also to Mervyn Barratt and Melior Whitear of the Information Department for much help and advice; to Owen Welles, publisher of the *NAPO Probation Directory*, for permission to use material from the directory in the book; to Nicky Vassall (the Women Prisoners' Resource Centre) for advice and for permission to use material from the 'Reception Pack'; to Alison Stanley and Sue Shutter (Joint Council for the Welfare of Immigrants); to Pat Moynihan (National Council for One-Parent Families); to Evette Powell (the Rastafarian Advisory Centre); to David Hale, press officer at the Home Office; to Gerry Brett (The New Bridge) for bringing me up to date on the work of voluntary associates (VAs); to Tim Owen, barrister, for painstakingly checking the legal sections of the manuscript; to Inga Keble-White (Good Offices) for her patience in helping with preparation of the manuscript; to my editor, Jackie Sallon, for her expert help and careful attention to detail; to all the other organisations listed who kindly sent me material and assisted with telephone enquiries; to James Anderson, prison governor and friend; to Roy Barr (my liaison probation officer during my years as a New Bridge VA) for all he taught me and for years of unfailing friendship and support; and finally to my 'clients', for the friendship they gave me during my 10 years as a practising VA.

Abbreviations in common prison use

LRC local review committee (attached to a given prison)
LDR last date of release
EDR estimated date of release
PED parole eligibility date
VO visiting order
VA voluntary associate (of the probation and after-care service)
HMP Her Majesty's pleasure (during Her Majesty's pleasure – an indeterminate sentence)

Part I
The Law

1 At the police station

Every citizen is regarded as having a civic duty to help police officers prevent crime and discover offenders, and a police officer is entitled to question any person who he or she thinks can give him useful information which might lead to an arrest. Therefore, it is important for everyone, however law–abiding, to know their rights in such a situation.

Being questioned by the police

You do not have to break the law to find yourself being asked questions by the police. Anyone (and in particular anyone related or closely connected to someone the police suspect of having committed a crime) may be asked to go to a police station to help the police or even find themselves under arrest.

When the police are looking for someone you know

If you are there when the police come to arrest someone related or known to you, be prepared for the possibility that they will question you, whether the person they are looking for is there or not. You don't have to answer questions if you don't want to, but it's sensible to be polite and to try to remain calm.

If the police go to arrest someone and find only their partner there when they arrive, they are likely to ask questions to try to find out where the suspected person is. They may ask about other matters as well. If you should be alone at home when police come to arrest your partner try to keep your cool. This may be difficult, especially if you have young children, but it's best to bear in mind that the children will be likely to take their

cue from you. If you panic it won't make the situation any
easier, and you may find yourself coping with tearful children
on top of your other problems.

How to get in touch with someone held at a police station

If someone closely connected with you is being held at a police
station you should try to get in touch with them as soon as
possible. If you don't know which police station they are being
held at you may have to ring around all the local police stations
and ask the custody officer in each one if the person you are
trying to contact is being held there.

There are a number of voluntary and self-help groups that
exist to help the families and partners of prisoners and they will
help you find out where someone is being held if you run into
difficulty. For more information about the various groups see
pages 89–91 and pages 186–92.

When you have found out where your friend or relative is
you should call and ask to see them. If they have not already
seen a solicitor contact one yourself (see page 7) and ask the
solicitor to call at the police station as soon as possible. If you
are told you cannot see your friend or relative then say you are
prepared to wait or that you will come back later.

If the person being held at the police station is in a special
category such as a juvenile, someone who is handicapped in
some way, an immigrant, foreign national or citizen of an
independent commonwealth country, or a refugee seeking
asylum, see pages 11–17.

Giving your name and address to a police officer

On the whole you are within your rights in refusing to give
your name and address to the police if they ask for it casually.
However, if you are stopped while in charge of a motor vehicle
or motor cycle, it is an offence to refuse to give your name and
address. But even when you are not under a legal obligation to
comply it may make the police suspicious if you refuse to co-
operate with their inquiries. They may get the idea that you
have something to hide or that you have committed an offence,
so if you refuse to give your name and address the police may
decide to arrest you anyway. The same applies if they suspect
that you have given them false information.

Going to the police station of your own free will

A person who goes to a police station voluntarily to help police officers with their inquiries is entitled to no less consideration than a suspect under arrest or being held for questioning. You have three basic rights:

1   the right to get in touch with someone outside the police station
2   the right to ask for legal advice
3   the right to see a copy of *The Codes of Practice* issued under an Act of Parliament in 1984

Rights 1 and 2 may be delayed under certain specific circumstances where offences of a serious nature are involved.

The Codes of Practice

The Codes of Practice are a detailed set of guidelines issued under the Police and Criminal Evidence Act 1984. This Act, which lawyers and police usually refer to familiarly as PACE, updated police procedure on arrest, detention and questioning at a police station. In this book, *The Codes of Practice* shall be called the *PACE Code*. It contains both statutory rules and advice for the police on every aspect of the way they should treat members of the public or suspects at a police station. It is a detailed document and not easy for a layperson to understand. If you decide you want to consult the *PACE Code* you may need the help of a friend or solicitor in sorting out the necessary information, especially if you are feeling under pressure. However, if you are alone at a police station and worried about your rights or how the police are treating you, ask to be shown in the *PACE Code* where exactly it says what the police should or should not do on a given matter.

There are special provisions in the *PACE Code* for treatment of juveniles, people who are mentally handicapped or mentally ill, deaf, blind or partially sighted persons, those unable to read, to speak, to understand English, citizens from the Commonwealth and foreign nationals. See pages 11–17 for further information. Immigrants, refugees, ethnic minority groups or anyone likely to be questioned about their residential status should see pages 12–17.

Rights of those who go to a police station voluntarily

If you have not been charged or placed under arrest you are free to leave when you wish. If told you cannot leave you should either be placed under arrest at once and taken before the custody officer or cautioned. In either case ask to see a solicitor immediately. It is your right. You are under no obligation to have fingerprints taken or allow your photograph to be taken.

Any person who goes to a police station voluntarily to assist police officers with their inquiries is entitled to be given writing materials if they wish. They may also speak on the telephone for a reasonable time to one person. In a 24–hour period at least two light meals and one main meal should be offered. Breaks for refreshment should be offered at approximately two–hourly intervals.

Arrest

General advice

In theory, if you are asked to go to the police station to answer questions and have not been placed under arrest you can refuse to go. However, the police might decide to arrest you anyway.

Once you have been placed under arrest you have no choice but to go along to the station to answer questions. Don't try to resist arrest by showing force or you may find yourself facing additional charges.

While it is important to remember to 'go quietly', you should also take steps to protect your interests, especially if you have reason to believe a serious charge is going to be made against you.

If you know in advance that the police are coming to arrest you, contact them and ask to meet them at a solicitor's office or ask a solicitor to go with you or to meet you at the police station. In an emergency try to get a friend or relative to go along with you so that they will know where you are being held.

The most important thing to remember once you have been placed under arrest is to get legal advice as quickly as possible. If you do not either know a solicitor or know where to contact one, there are organisations that can help you. See page 8.

The arrest procedure and your rights

At the time of arrest you should be cautioned (unless you have been cautioned immediately beforehand). A caution is given in the following words: 'You do not have to say anthing unless you wish to do so but what you say may be given in evidence.' Once you are under arrest you have the right to remain silent and to get legal advice.

On arrival at the police station you will be told your three basic rights:

1   to have someone outside the police station told of your arrest
2   to consult a solicitor
3   to see a copy of the *PACE Code*

Don't worry if you have second thoughts after having said you don't want anyone told of your arrest, or don't want to see a solicitor, because you also have the right to change your mind.

Getting legal advice at a police station

You can ask the police to contact your own solicitor at any time while you are at a police station, or you can ask them to contact one you know of. If no solicitor known to you is available there are other options open to you. No one who is at a police station and wants legal advice should have to go without it. Once you tell the police that you want legal advice you should not be kept waiting except in certain serious cases, and then only with the agreement of the superintendant. You should, in any case, not have to wait longer than 36 hours from the time you arrived at the police station, or 48 hours in terrorism cases.

Once you have asked for legal advice you should not be asked further questions until you have spoken to a solicitor.

If you do not know of a solicitor you can ask the police to contact the duty solicitor. The duty solicitor scheme operates 24 hours a day on a rota basis. The duty solicitor, who is independent of the police, is paid under the legal aid scheme and you will not have to pay anything nor will you be asked questions about your means.

If you can't get hold of your own solicitor or one that you know of, and don't want to see the duty solicitor, ask the police for a list of local solicitors. They will ring round until they find someone on the list who is able to attend. You will not have to pay as solicitors are paid under the legal aid scheme for the time they spend helping anyone at a police station.

You (or someone else on your behalf) can also find a solicitor through your local citizens advice bureau (CAB) or other advice agency. In particular Release, an independent advice agency, provides a free advice service for anyone in trouble with the law and they have a 24–hour legal helpline. For this telephone number and their address and daytime office number see page 180. Release can supply names and addresses of local solicitors and many of their legal workers are solicitors. See also pages 181–92 for how to get in touch with other advice agencies.

Copies of free leaflets about legal aid can be obtained from the town hall, library, CAB or law centre or by writing direct to the Central Office of Information (see page 180). Head your letter 'Home Office Publications (A)'.

Police bail

As soon as the police have finished questioning a suspect they should release or charge them. Once charged the suspect can ask for bail. Bail means being allowed to go free between arrest (or being charged or both) and another visit to the police station for further questioning or appearing in court.

Police bail can be refused for any one of the following reasons:

The police believe that the suspect

- will not turn up for trial, or at the police station
- is likely to interfere with witnesses
- is likely to re–offend

The more serious the offence, the less likely the police are to grant bail.

When bail is refused the suspect will be kept in custody until the first available court date which should be the following morning. At weekends or bank holidays court appearances may be delayed.

Unconditional bail

The police can only release a suspect on unconditional bail. If they want to make bail conditions they must take the suspect before a magistrates' court and ask for certain conditions, such as a condition of residency or a surety (see page 22), to be attached to the granting of bail.

For details of court bail see page 22.

Custody procedure and your rights

Once you have been taken to the police station under arrest (or, having gone of your own free will, are arrested there), a police officer, known as the custody officer, will write on a form everything to do with your case. This form is known as the custody record.

After you have been cautioned, the custody officer will tell you why you are being held and ask you to sign the custody record to note whether or not you have asked for legal advice. If you disagree with anything written on the custody record you can and should refuse to sign it when invited to do so. If you do refuse to sign, the custody officer will note this on the custody record.

You (or your legal representative) have the right to ask for a copy of your custody record when you leave the police station. You can ask for it up to 12 months after the time you leave the police station.

Once you are released from custody you (or your legal representative) can ask to see the original custody record. Allow a reasonable time for it to be produced.

A suspect in custody should not

- be forced to answer questions (you have the right to remain silent)
- be forced to make a statement against their will
- be induced to make a statement by means of threats or by being promised something, such as bail, for instance. (Statements that have not been made freely may be inadmissable as evidence in court.)

No person who has been charged should be asked further questions except in certain exceptional circumstances. (Ask to see the *PACE Code*).

Time limits for police custody

No one should be held for more than 24 hours before being charged. However, in certain serious cases (ask to see the *PACE Code* if this applies to you), this can be extended a further 12 hours to a total of 36 hours. If the police wish to hold anyone longer for questioning they must go before a magistrate to ask for a further 36 hours. Evidence in later court proceedings may be declared inadmissable if the accused person was held for longer than 48 hours.

In cases which come under the Prevention of Terrorism (Temporary Provisions) Act 1984, suspects can be held for up to seven days with the authorisation of the Home Secretary. In such cases, the right not to be held incommunicado or to have access to legal advice may be delayed for as long as a senior officer considers necessary, but not longer than 48 hours after arrest.

Being taken before a magistrate

Once someone has been charged they should be taken before a magistrates' court as soon as practicable. If it is not practicable to bring a suspect before magistrates within 24 hours they should be released on bail. This may not apply if the offence is serious. In this case 48 hours may elapse before the suspect is taken before a court.

Rights of suspects under arrest

You can ask to see a solicitor at any time even if you have previously said you did not want to. You can also speak on the telephone for a reasonable time to one person and ask them to come and see you. The police may only delay either of these rights if you have been charged with a serious offence, and then only in certain specific circumstances. Ask to see the *PACE Code*. You should be given writing materials if you ask for them. You may ask to see a doctor. You may if you wish ask to see a doctor of your own choice at your own expense. If you have medicine with you for a heart condition, diabetes, epilepsy (or any other serious condition), or if you need such medicine, you should be allowed to see a doctor as soon as possible.

In a 24-hour period at least two light meals and one main meal should be offered. Breaks for refreshment should also be made at approximately 2-hourly intervals.

Intimate body searches

An intimate body search may only be carried out if there are reasons for believing that an article which could cause physical injury to the detained person or others at the police station has been concealed or drugs have been concealed. A detained person should be told why an intimate body search is considered necessary before it is carried out.

An intimate body search

- may only be carried out by a person of the same sex who should be a doctor, state registered nurse (SRN), or state enrolled nurse (see the *PACE Code* for the circumstances where a superintendent or more senior officer may dispense with this rule)
- should only take place at a hospital, surgery, other medical premises or at a police station
- should not be carried out in the presence of any person of the opposite sex (other than a qualified doctor or nurse) or any person whose presence is unnecessary

In the case of a juvenile, mentally ill or mentally handicapped person, a suitable adult of the same sex must be present (see below) unless the juvenile or persons as above and adult agree otherwise.

Juveniles in custody

Anyone under 17 years of age is classed as a juvenile. A juvenile who is arrested or taken to a police station for questioning should have a 'suitable adult' (defined below) at the police station with them while they are being questioned or charged. The *PACE Code* states that this should be arranged 'as soon as practicable'. The adult can be a parent, guardian or social worker. A juvenile in care may have someone from the care authority such as a social worker. If none of these are available (or the person available is thought unsuitable for some good reason), some other responsible adult should be called. This should not be a police officer or anyone employed by the police.

The custody officer should contact the adult as soon as possible to let them know why the juvenile has been detained and where they are being held, and should then ask the adult to come to the police station. The juvenile should be told their rights in the presence of the adult if they are already at the police station, and again after the adult has arrived if they are not.

When the juvenile leaves detention, the adult (or legal representative) can ask for a copy of the custody record. The original custody record should also be available for inspection by the adult or lawyer.

When a juvenile is the subject of a supervision order the person supervising should be told as soon as possible.

Duties of an adult assisting a juvenile in custody

The adult should not just watch but should advise the young person and help them to communicate with the police. It is also their duty to make sure the interview is being properly and fairly conducted.

No young person should be arrested at a school or college unless this is unavoidable. In such a case the principal or a suitable adult (see above) should be present.

The custody officer should try to make arrangements for a juvenile who is kept in custody after being charged to be taken into the care of the local authority until the time of the court appearance.

An intimate search of a juvenile at a police station should only take place in the presence of an adult (see above) who, in this instance, must be of the same sex as the juvenile concerned.

People with special needs in custody

When a person who is mentally handicapped or mentally ill is being questioned or charged a suitable adult should be present to help them. This may be either a relative or guardian, or some person used to dealing with the mentally ill who may not be either a police officer or employed by the police. The custody officer should get in touch with the chosen adult as soon as possible and ask them to come to the police station. Otherwise follow the guidance as for juveniles on page 11.

When people who are blind, partially sighted or unable to read are in custody, a solicitor, relative or suitable adult (not someone in the police or employed by the police) should be present to help in checking documentation and to sign for the detained person (with their consent) when appropriate.

Anyone who is either deaf, hard of hearing, or who for other reasons cannot communicate with the custody officer is entitled to the assistance of an interpreter. Most social services departments have lists of suitable interpreters.

Advice for non-UK citizens, refugees and members of ethnic minority groups

If you are black, from overseas, or visibly from an ethnic minority group, you are statistically more likely to be stopped by the police and questioned than a person who is not. If you are stopped by the police you are quite likely to find yourself being questioned on your residence status in the UK. Be prepared for this as you may be stopped for something relatively minor such as a traffic offence. However, the police have no right to question you in this way unless they have reason to believe you have committed an immigration offence. (If you are an immigrant, or if your residential status is in any doubt, see below). Whatever your nationality or immigration status you should take legal advice if you are charged with an offence. You are entitled to apply for legal aid (see page 21). If you are a refugee and want to claim political asylum you should get specialised advice as quickly as possible. If you are a citizen of an independent commonwealth country or a foreign national, see below.

Arrest or questioning of independent Commonwealth citizens or foreign nationals at a police station

The above may communicate at any time with their High Commission, embassy or consulate (including the Republic of Ireland).

A Commonwealth citizen detained for more than 24 hours is entitled to be told why they are being kept in custody and to have the reasons for their detention and their whereabouts passed on by the police to their High Commission if they so wish.

Any foreign national may communicate with their consul or have information about their arrest passed on to consular officials by the police.

Political refugees have the right to refuse to have their consul told of their whereabouts.

Arrest or questioning of immigrants at a police station

If you are arrested do not say anything except to give your name and address. You should immediately take legal advice (see page 7).

The *PACE Code* (see page 5) applies to you *to a limited extent* while you are in police custody, but if immigration officers are called in they will use their own Code of Practice.

Give only your name, date of birth and nationality but nothing else until you have received advice. If you are in any doubt ask to phone a friend and ask him or her to seek advice on your behalf from one of the agencies listed on pages 133–4, or to find you a solicitor who is experienced in immigration cases. For how to contact your local law centre, see pages 134–8.

If you do have to appear in court ask to see a probation officer. The probation service have produced a booklet in 20 languages giving details about what happens in court, and a booklet for prisoners in 15 languages.

The police may decide not to charge you with a criminal offence but to let immigration officers deal with the matter of immigration. If you do not hold British nationality you may be liable to deportation or removal. If this applies to you see below.

Interpreters

A person detained in police custody who has difficulty in understanding English is entitled to have the assistance of an interpreter at public expense. The interpreter should explain the alleged offence and pass on any other information given by the custody officer.

Deportation of immigrants and others

If any of the following apply to you seek advice immediately from your nearest law centre as you may be vulnerable to deportation:

● You have overstayed your legal entitlement to stay in this country.
● You have broken a condition on your stay (for example, by working without permission).
● You have been recommended for deportation by a court.
● The Home Office have grounds to believe that to deport you would be 'conducive to the public good'.
● You are the wife (or child aged under 18) of any of the above.

Immunity from deportation

You are immune to deportation only if you are:

● a British citizen
● a Commonwealth citizen with 'right of abode'. (This means that you are not subject to British immigration control

because either you had a parent born in the UK, or because
you are a woman who married a man who had the right of
abode *and* you married before 1 January 1983)
- a Commonwealth citizen who had been given the right to
stay permanently in this country before 1 January 1973 and
had been living here for a period of not less than five years
since that date. (If you were resident in this country from 1
January 1973 you are not immune and could be deported)

Right to appeal against deportation

You have a full right of appeal (and the right to put forward
compassionate grounds in support of your claim) only if you
have been living in the UK for seven years before a decision
was made to deport you. If you have been living here less than
seven years (and acting illegally), the scope of your right of
appeal is limited. You can only challenge the power *in law* of
the Secretary of State to deport you and appeal on the specific
facts of your overstaying. No compassionate grounds against
deportation can be considered.

In theory, you also have the right to appeal against being sent
to a particular country. This is known as a 'destination appeal'.
However, in practice this right is of little value except in the
case of a person who is refused asylum in this country but who
might be accepted by a country other than their own.

Removal of illegal entrants

You are classed as an illegal entrant and can be 'removed' by
the British government if any of the following apply to you:

- You entered the UK by any sort of 'deception'. This can
mean that you failed to tell the immigration officer
something or that someone else told the officer something
that was untrue either about you or about your
circumstances. For example, you did not tell the immigration
officer that you were married to someone in the UK.
- You were not frank about your intentions. For example, you
said that you were staying for a week when you were in fact
intending to stay and work or study. This could be held
against you.
- When you entered the UK you did so without passing
through immigration control.

Right to appeal against removal

There is no right of appeal against removal from the UK while you are still here, only after you have been sent back, but you may be able to go to the High Court for a judicial review of the Secretary of State's decision. In this case you should seek expert legal advice from a lawyer specialising in immigration law. Consult the JCWI (Joint Council for the Welfare of Immigrants) or your local law centre (see pages 182–6).

Advice for immigrants facing a charge

If you are taken before a court and convicted (and do not have immunity from deportation), you may find yourself in either of the following situations: your deportation is recommended by a court, or the Home Office decides to deport you. If deportation is recommended by a court as part of a sentence there is no right of appeal except through the criminal justice system. However, you do have the right of appeal against 'destination' (see above), but you must lodge an appeal within 28 days of the court's ruling or you will lose your right to appeal. Even if the court has recommended deportation the Home Office will not automatically deport you. Shortly before your release date (EDR) the Home Office will write to you asking if there is any reason why you should not be deported. It is important to write back immediately and give full details.

Even if deportation is not recommended by the court, the Home Office can still decide to deport you if you are not settled here, or if they decide it is 'not conducive to the public good' for you to remain in this country.

If the Home Office decide to deport you without a court having made such a recommendation, the procedure is similar, but in that instance you can make representation. If they still decide on deportation, you then also have 'right of appeal', but you must lodge an appeal within 14 days from service of notice.

You are entitled to legal aid for the preparation of an appeal but not for representation. Consult a solicitor (see page 8) or your local law centre (see pages 182–6). Immigrants can get representation through a government-funded agency, UKIAS (United Kingdom Immigrants Advisory Service) which was set up to advise and represent people in immigration appeals (see page 182).

Advice for immigrants leaving the UK summarily

If you are unsuccessful in appeal, have no right of appeal or want to go home as quickly as possible, then it is important that you (or someone else on your behalf checks out that your passport is both available and in order. You may also want to take the precaution of booking a ticket home.

Caution for immigrants leaving the UK summarily

If any of the above apply and you do not make arrangements for leaving the UK immediately, you may find yourself spending further time in a remand wing awaiting deportation (see pages 36–40 for details about remand).

Where immigration detainees are held

- at detention centres. Harmondsworth, near Heathrow, is the largest, and there are also centres near most major seaports or airports
- a deportation wing at Latchmere House Remand Centre (Richmond). However, this is due to be moved to Haslar in Hampshire in the near future
- remand wings of most prisons
- police stations

Advice for refugees

All refugees should get proper advice as soon as possible. Any of the categories of people discussed above may also have a claim to refugee status and asylum and this could include:

- those convicted of a criminal offence
- people who have 'overstayed' or are working in breach of their conditions of stay
- illegal entrants

Any of the above are in potential danger of becoming prisoners under the Immigration Act 1971 and should seek specialised advice as quickly as possible (see pages 181–2).

Making a complaint about the police

Complaints about the police should be referred immediately to your solicitor. (If you don't know a solicitor, see page 7). You could, in addition, consult the following advice agencies, each of which has a specific function which might be helpful in your case (for how to contact them, see pages 180–92):

Justice will give advice at the point of referral though they are mainly concerned with individual casework on cases of alleged wrongful conviction.

The *National Council for Civil Liberties* provides legal advice on all aspects of the criminal justice system, especially in so far as civil liberties have been violated.

Inquest campaigns in the area of deaths in custody.

Other advice agencies.   Most of the advice agencies who help prisoners or their partners would give you initial advice or refer you to where you might obtain the most appropriate advice.

Police Complaints Authority.   You can also write to the chairman of the Police Complaints Authority giving the facts of your case and asking for it to be investigated.

If you have been charged the next step is to appear before a magistrates' court. If you have not been given police bail it is up to the police to take you to court. If you have been allowed bail then it is up to you to turn up at the court on the correct date and time. It is an offence not to answer to your bail. When you arrive at the court you should report to the goaler's office as soon as possible.

2 The magistrates' court

Magistrates' courts try and sentence less serious types of cases. The longest prison sentence they can pass is up to 6 months. However, they may pass consecutive sentences up to a maximum of 12 months.

Magistrates' courts act as a filter through which more serious criminal cases pass before going on to be heard by the Crown Court. They also make crucial decisions about whether or not a defendant should be granted bail or remanded to prison to await trial. They can commit a convicted person to a Crown Court for sentence if they feel that the offence merits a longer sentence than they are able to impose. They can also pass non-custodial sentences when they consider this to be more appropriate than sending someone to prison, and they have a wide range of such options.

Where a defendant has been given bail to appear in court they should report to the gaoler's office as soon as possible.

Why legal help is necessary

It is unwise for anyone appearing before a court on a criminal charge not to have the help of a solicitor. You should not, on any account, plead 'guilty' without first taking legal advice. You might believe yourself to be guilty but legal advice may show that you are not or that you are guilty of a different or a lesser offence. If in doubt it is always safest to plead 'not guilty' to a charge as this can be changed after consulting a lawyer, whereas a 'guilty' plea cannot be altered except in exceptional circumstances.

Emergency advice for anyone appearing in court

1   Do not plead 'guilty' without first taking legal
    advice.
    You may believe that you are guilty but legal advice
    may show that you are not or that you are guilty of
    a different or a lesser offence.
       If in any doubt about what to plead it is safest to
    plead 'not guilty' as this plea can be changed after
    getting legal advice, whereas a guilty plea is more
    difficult to change.

2   Ask for bail (see page 22).
    Remember that a friend, relative or some suitable
    person known to you may be needed in court to
    act as surety (see pages 22–3).

3   Get legal advice (see below).
    If your solicitor does not turn up for any reason,
    ask to have the case adjourned.
       If English is not your native language have a
    word with the probation officer at the court. The
    probation service have produced a booklet in 20
    different languages about what happens in court
    and your language might be one of them.

The duty solicitor

Most courts operate the duty solicitor scheme. If you have not
seen a solicitor already ask court staff as soon as you arrive if
you can see the duty solicitor. The duty solicitor's advice and
help will be free and he or she can advise you about the
following matters:
● bail
● getting your case put off to another day
● whether you should plead 'guilty' or 'not guilty'
● getting your own solicitor and applying for criminal legal
  aid
● the sentence you might be expected to get
● any other problems about your case

The duty solicitor can also represent you when you first go in
front of the magistrates.

Remember, if your solicitor does not turn up, or there is no duty solicitor, you can always apply to have the case adjourned to give you time to get proper legal advice.

Legal aid for criminal offences

Legal aid is available for those who either cannot afford to pay at all or cannot afford to pay the whole bill. Anyone who has been charged with, or has received a summons for, a criminal offence has the right to apply for legal aid.

For information on how the legal aid scheme works, see below.

How can legal aid help me? Legal aid will pay for a solicitor to prepare your case before you go to court and then to represent you in court. If your case goes to a Crown Court it will also cover the cost of a barrister.

Is legal aid entirely free? Legal aid will either help you to pay for the case or cover the entire cost. How much you pay and how much the court pays depend on what you can afford. If you pay something and then are acquitted later you will probably get back what you have paid.

How do I get legal aid? Apply to the court which is hearing your case. You will have to fill in an application form and another form giving details of your income and savings. The forms can be obtained either from the court or from your solicitor.

Can I get help in filling in the forms? A solicitor (your own or the duty solicitor) can help you fill in the forms.

How can I be sure to get legal aid if I need it? Help yourself by telling the court why you need a solicitor. If the court decides that you need help to pay a solicitor to defend you and that your case is serious enough to merit a possible prison sentence, you will be granted legal aid. Other considerations might be that there are legal or other complications or that you might lose your job if found guilty.

When should I apply for legal aid? Apply as soon as possible after you have been charged or received a summons for a criminal offence. You may apply at any time before your case is heard but the sooner you apply the more time your solicitor will have to prepare your case.

Can I make more than one application for legal aid? There is no limit to the number of applications you can make.

Copies of free leaflets about legal aid can be obtained from your local town hall, library, CAB or law centre, or by writing direct to the Central Office of Information. Head your letter 'Home Office Publications (A)' (see page 180). For further information on getting legal help see pages 7–8.

Court bail

Court bail means being allowed to go free between the time of the first court appearance (and any subsequent court appearances) and the trial.

Bail is generally only refused if the magistrate has substantial grounds for believing the suspect will either fail to turn up for the trial, will commit further offences or interfere with witnesses. However, bail can also be refused sometimes 'in the best interests of the defendant'. This would apply especially in a case involving a juvenile under 16 in order to 'protect the welfare of the child'.

It is up to the court to decide whether to grant bail, and if it is granted, whether to make it subject to certain conditions. The more serious the offence the less likely it is that bail will be granted. Conditions might be that the suspect agrees to stay at a particular address, hand over a passport or that the suspect can produce a surety.

It is an offence not to turn up to answer bail at the correct time without a very good reason (such as being taken ill or admitted to hospital) and can result in immediate arrest.

Acting as a surety

Sometimes when bail is granted a condition might be imposed that some person who knows the suspect guarantees a sum of money to ensure that the suspect will turn up at court at the correct date and time. This person, called a 'surety', must be aged over 18, have a permanent address, be employed and have no criminal record. It is not necessary to be a relative to act as a surety.

How much money is involved? The court decides on the amount and this will generally depend on how serious the offence is and how much risk there is of the suspect failing to turn up to answer bail.

When does the surety have to hand over money? No money has to be handed over in advance and the surety does not have to take the money to the police station or court. However, the police or the court will want to make sure that the surety can produce the agreed sum of money at short notice, if necessary.

Does the surety always lose money if the suspect defaults? This is a matter for the court to decide. The magistrate will want some assurance that the surety is likely to be able to get the suspect back to court when called. If the suspect fails to turn up the surety may lose some or all of the money they guaranteed. It is up to the surety to keep the police informed. If there is any likelihood of the suspect running away the surety should at once inform the police or they will almost certainly lose money and may even be arrested.

Information for friends or relatives

If you are going to court to give support to a partner, relative or friend, check the time a particular case is likely to be heard by consulting the list for that day. You will usually find it pinned up on a wall in the main lobby. Arrive by 9.45 am to allow time to check, as most courts start at 10 am. If you are in doubt about when a case is to be heard, ask the police officer who is in charge of making sure the list runs smoothly. If you wish to check the next day's list in advance, telephone the court on the afternoon before. You may have to do this several times.

If you want to see someone in the cells before the case is heard (you might want to check that they have a solicitor and, if not, to offer to contact one), ask the gaoler or the court probation officer. Check whether they have had legal advice. If not, try and get them a solicitor (see pages 7–8). You may also be able to act as a surety if they are given bail (see page 22). Visitors can sit in the public gallery.

The probation officer has access to the cells and should be able to pass on an important message for you if necessary. Ask the court usher to point out the probation officer to you.

What happens first

When a case comes to a magistrates' court, there are three important decisions to be made. The first is whether the case will be tried there or referred to a Crown Court. This will be determined by the type of offence. The most serious offences such as murder, robbery or rape can only be tried by a Crown

Court. Some offences can *only* be tried summarily by a magistrates' court. Some offences can be tried by either court and when this applies:

- either the defence may elect to go for trial by jury at a Crown Court or
- the Crown Prosecution Service (CPS) may decide that the case should be tried by the higher court or
- the magistrates themselves may decide the case is too serious for them to try

If it is decided that the case should go to the higher court, the next step is to set the date of the committal proceedings. If, however, the case is to be heard at the magistrates' court, the defence has to decide upon their plea. If the plea is 'guilty', the case is heard there and then. If the plea is 'not guilty', it will have to be adjourned for a full hearing. The date for this will be set to allow both sides to prepare and present their evidence.

Procedure when the offence can be tried in either a magistrates' court or a Crown Court

The clerk of the court will stand and inform the defendant of his or her rights in the following words:

The magistrate has decided that your case is more suitable for trial at this court. However, before you finally decide whether you would like to be tried here, you should know that you have a right to be tried by a judge and jury at a Crown Court. However, if you consent to be tried by this court and you either plead guilty or are found guilty then the magistrate may still commit you for sentence to the Crown Court if, after hearing about your character or after hearing of any previous convictions you may have, he feels that his own powers of punishment are not enough. Where do you wish to be tried?

The defendant can now say either: 'I would like this court to go ahead and hear my case', or 'I would like to consult a solicitor before I answer these questions' or 'I would prefer to be tried by a judge and jury at a Crown Court.'

If the plea is guilty the case goes ahead and sentence is passed. If the plea is 'not guilty' the case will be adjourned for a full hearing.

At the full hearing the court will hear the evidence and decide whether the case has been found 'proven' or 'not proven'. If the case against the defendant is found not proven it ends there and the defendant can go home. If the case is found proven the CPS lawyer will pass on details of any previous convictions to assist the court in deciding what sentence to pass.

When it is time to pass sentence, the court may decide (if the case is serious enough and bearing in mind magistrates can only pass a sentence of six months) to refer the case to a Crown Court for sentencing. A further option open to the court is to impose a non-custodial sentence instead of a prison sentence.

Sentencing

Providing positive help at time of sentencing

The more evidence that can be presented to the court to show that the offender wishes to make a fresh start and stay out of trouble, the better the chances of avoiding a custodial sentence. Back-up from a partner or family is important, especially if they can be in court to demonstrate their support.

Where an offender has no partner or close family a good relationship with a VA (voluntary associate) may be seen as an acceptable alternative. A VA who has known an offender for some time can also act as a 'character witness'. Courts are well aware that an isolated single person stands a greater chance of re-offending than someone who can count on support when the going gets rough. See pages 58–60 to find out about VAs and what they can do to help offenders.

It is in the offender's interests to make sure that the probation officer knows about every possible positive factor in their case. Where there has not been a previous link, this is more important than ever since the court probation officer is likely to be very busy and have many other cases on hand. Remember that the officer is not *representing* the offender in writing a report for the court, but merely presenting the court with information to aid its sentencing function.

It can form an important part of any defence to show that an offender may be able to take part in one of the schemes described below or has the offer of a place at an appropriate hostel if the offence is linked to alcohol or drug dependancy.

Passing sentence

An offender who is found guilty at a magistrates' court will either receive a short prison sentence (either less than 6 months or consecutive sentences of not more than 12 months) or a non-custodial sentence.

Prison is an extremely expensive option, both in terms of

how much it costs the public purse and in its effect on the lives
not only of convicted persons but also on the lives of their
partners and families. Of course, a major factor in sentencing
must always be whether or not the offender is considered a
danger to the community at large. Successive Home Secretaries
have stressed the necessity of using imprisonment only as a last
resort, when the court considers that none of the available non-
custodial sentences is suitable. Yet, in spite of this and in spite
of the wide range of non-custodial sentences available to the
courts, their use has declined over the last decade. Also, for
some reason women defendants do not seem to be offered the
same range of options as men.

Before passing sentence courts will take into account the
seriousness of the offence, the offender's previous convictions
and personal circumstances as well as any mitigating
circumstances. Social inquiry reports (sometimes called
probation reports) or medical reports may be called for to
present a fuller picture. There are no minimum sentences, but
some offences carry maximum sentences and certain road traffic
offences carry mandatory sentences.

Non-custodial sentences

Absolute discharge. This may be given when a court which has
found an offender guilty of an offence considers that no further
action is necessary.

Conditional discharge. Like an absolute discharge, a conditional
discharge places no obligation on the offender. However, if a
further offence is committed within a specified period of not
more than three years, the offender may then be sentenced for
the original offence.

Deferred sentence. The court postpones the passing of sentence
for a period of time on various specified conditions including
that the defendant commits no further offence.

Bind over. A court can bind someone over to keep the peace or
be of good behaviour for a specified period. The court fixes a
sum of money and if the offender breaches the undertaking,
they may be required to forfeit some or all of the money.

Suspended sentence. This is a sentence of imprisonment which is
fixed only to be served in the event of the offender committing
a further offence during the period of suspension.

Fines

Any criminal offence (except murder) can be punished by the
imposition of a fine. Courts are obliged to take the offender's
means into account when imposing a fine. When a court
decides that a fine is the most suitable punishment for a child
or young person under the age of 17, their parent or guardian
will have to pay the fine unless either they cannot be found or
circumstances make this unreasonable. Failure to pay a fine can
result in imprisonment, but generally other methods of getting
the fine paid will be used before this. For instance, time to pay
may be extended; the size or frequency, or both, of instalment
payments may be varied; 'distraint' (seizure) of the offender's
goods may be ordered; and an attachment of earnings order, a
money payment supervision order, or an attendance centre
order may be made.

Compensation and restitution orders

These are often used in conjunction with another sentence
although they can be used on their own. The court can order an
offender to pay compensation in respect of personal injury, loss
or damage resulting from the offence. Where goods have been
stolen, the courts may impose a restitution order. This means
that the offender must restore the goods to the owner (or
anything bought with the proceeds of the sale of the goods). If
both a fine and restitution order would be appropriate, but the
offender has insufficient means to pay both, the court should
give the compensation order precedence. The same procedures
are available to courts for enforcement as for fines.

Probation

A probation order (which can only be made with the full
consent and co-operation of the defendant) can be for a period
of between six months and three years. It is only available for
offenders aged 17 and over. The aim of probation is to keep the
offender at liberty in the community while, to some extent,
controlling his or her behaviour and helping to overcome the
problems which led to the offence being committed in the first
place. Generally a probation order includes certain
requirements. Usually these will be that the offender agrees to
lead a good and industrious life and keep the probation officer
informed of any change of address or employment. Regular
reporting at stipulated times and visits at home as required by

the probation officer are also fairly general. Other, more specialised requirements can include undergoing psychiatric treatment, attending a day centre for a specified period of up to 60 days or living at a probation hostel (or other specified place) for a period of any length of time up to completion of the probation order.

Community service orders

A community service order entails doing unpaid work in the community for a total of anything between 40 and 240 hours in a 12-month period (120 hours for those under 16), and can be imposed upon any person aged 16 or over who has been convicted of an imprisonable offence. The probation service oversee the work and a breach may result in the offender being taken back to court where they can be fined for the breach or resentenced for the original offence.

Drug or alcohol recovery project hostels

Courts may make residence at a drug or alcohol recovery project a condition of probation. The problem with this is that project workers generally regard the commitment of the ex-offender as paramount if they are to be able to make a success of taking part in this type of project. Imposition of residence by the courts is not seen as helpful since the individual concerned must have a strong motivation to succeed in programmes that inevitably carry a degree of stress. Where such a scheme may be appropriate, a probation officer can advise about suitable and available projects.

Attendance centres

The maximum order is currently for 36 hours. This may be spread over a six-month period with the offender attending two or three days a week. Between the ages of 17–21 the order can be for 24 hours. Juveniles can be sentenced to a total of 12 hours. The full range of juvenile sentences is dealt with on pages 31–5.

What happens after sentence has been pronounced?

If a non-custodial sentence has been passed the offender can go home. If, however, a custodial or prison sentence has been given, the convicted prisoner will then be taken below to the cells to await transport to the prison where the sentence will begin.

After court has finished for the day it is sometimes possible to see a prisoner in the cells. Ask the solicitor acting in the case, or failing that, the gaoler at the court. Failing either of these ask the court probation officer. At the least the probation officer should be able to pass on a message for you.

Finding out where a newly sentenced person will be sent

The gaoler might know, so ask him. You should receive a letter from your partner within a few days.

The Police Holding Unit at Scotland Yard can tell you which prison recently admitted prisoners have been sent to (see page 190). You can telephone the unit but you may have to hang on for an answer for a long time.

If you can't find out at the court and don't want to wait for a letter and don't want to have to hang on the telephone for a long time, contact one of the organisations for prisoner's wives. See pages 89–91 to find out more about them and turn to pages 186–92 for how to get in touch. You can be sure of a friendly and warm welcome from any of them. There are several self-help groups where you will be sure to meet people who understand because they've been through the same thing themselves. They will help relatives, partners or close friends of a prisoner. Most of them will undertake to ring around for you, not just locally, but anywhere in the country.

From the magistrates' court an offender might be placed on remand (see pages 36–40) or they might be committed for trial at a Crown Court.

3 The juvenile court

It is impossible to consider the treatment of children and young people who offend without making mention of the children who appear in court as victims, since it is now widely recognised that the child victim of today is all too likely to be the offender of tomorrow.

Child victims who appear in court as witnesses suffer a second time by having to come to court to give evidence. Often they must come face to face with the very person who has attacked or abused them. However, screens are now sometimes used in court to allow young people to give evidence, secluded from the gaze of their abusers, and there has also been a trial use of videos to save young victims from having to appear in person. Child care experts are constantly looking at new ways of tackling this problem and of saving children who have been ill-treated from further trauma.

The age of criminal responsibility

Ten is considered to be the age of criminal responsibility. No child under 10 may be charged with an offence under any circumstances. Persistent or alleged offenders under the age of 10 can be dealt with as being beyond parental control. The police have the power to detain any child under a place of safety order.

Between the ages of 10 and 14 there is a presumption in law that children do not know right from wrong. If the prosecution bring a case involving a child aged between 10 and 14 it is for them to rebut this presumption.

Young people between the ages of 10 and 14 must be dealt

with summarily in the juvenile court. Summary trial means a trial which can take place only in a magistrates' or juvenile court. The only exceptions to this are cases of homicide or where a juvenile is charged jointly with an adult.

Young people over 14

It is assumed that young people between the ages of 14 and 16 are aware of the law and know right from wrong. They are classed as juveniles and appear at a special juvenile court where they must be dealt with summarily by magistrates. No juvenile can appear before an adult court unless they are either charged with homicide or charged in conjunction with an adult, or unless they are committed for trial on a serious indictable offence. Reports on juveniles are prepared by a social worker from the local authority or by a probation officer.

Young people over 17

Children cease to be classed as juveniles once they reach 17 and can appear before an adult court. Between the ages of 17 and 21 a juvenile is classed as a 'young offender'. Technically 'youth custody' no longer exists and 'young offenders' are detained in 'young offender institutions'. A magistrate who deals with a young offender has a wide range of options to consider before deciding to impose a custodial sentence.

Use of custodial and non-custodial sentences for juveniles and young offenders

Today government studies, as well as common sense, reflect the view which has long been held by those working in the field of prison reform. They believe that it makes little sense to put ever-increasing numbers of people in prison, at great expense to the community, only to release them after short periods, less able than ever to deal with the problems that got them into trouble in the first place. In the case of children and young people this problem is even more acute.

However, the problem remains of what to do with juveniles and young people who offend. Boys of 15 represent the largest group of offenders nationwide. New types of non-custodial sentences are constantly being studied and proposed and today there is a wider range than ever before of non-custodial sentences available to courts dealing with young offenders. In care cases there is often a very narrow line between children who are brought before the court for their own protection and children who begin a pattern of offending. Neither problem can be looked at in isolation.

Care orders for juveniles

Place of safety order. Anyone may apply for such an order in respect of a child or young person for a period not exceeding 28 days. A shorter period is more usual. An order obtained in out-of-court hours may not be given until the next day. The onus is then on the local authority to produce evidence for an extension. The place of safety order is regarded as an emergency measure to be used where a young person is actually at risk and court proceedings are being seriously considered. The person applying for a place of safety order must have reasonable cause for believing that the child or young person is in need of care or control and that one of the conditions of the Children and Young Persons Act 1969 applies.

Remand in care. A remand in care can only be made in respect of a juvenile offender. Where a juvenile has been arrested and the case has been heard initially in court but bail has not been granted, they will be remanded into the care of the local authority for the area in which they live. Similarly, if the juvenile has no settled address (or it is not known), they will be remanded into the care of the local authority where the alleged offence was committed. The maximum remand before finding of guilt is eight days. The maximum remand after finding of guilt is three weeks.

An adult co-defendant may elect to have their case tried before a judge and jury. If it is not possible to 'split' the case and deal separately with the young person in a juvenile court, the young person will be sent for trial with the adult. If the young offender is not granted bail they will be remanded in care for trial.

Secure accommodation order. Such an order may be considered necesssary

- where a young person being remanded to care has been charged or found guilty of an offence which would be imprisonable for a young person of 14 or more, and if they have been found guilty (or previously found guilty) of a violent offence

- where a young person is already in the care of a local authority or has a history of absconding and is likely to abscond from any other type of accommodation, and it is likely that their physical, mental or moral welfare may be at risk in the event of their absconding

Remand in custody (certificate of unruliness). When juveniles appear in court they should not be remanded in custody unless the court certifies that they are of so unruly a character that they cannot safely be committed to the care of a local authority. This can only apply to male juveniles aged over 15, but there are strict conditions governing the court's powers. These are:

- The young person is charged with an offence which in the case of an adult would be punishable with imprisonment of 14 years plus, and
  - (a) the court is remanding them for the first time in the proceedings; and is satisfied that there has not been time for the local authority to obtain a written report on the availability of accommodation in a community home or
  - (b) the court is satisfied (on the basis of a report) that no suitable accommodation is available in a community home without substantial risk to the young person or others.
- The young person is charged with or was found guilty of an offence of violence on a previous occasion and either of the above also applies.
- The young person has either persistently absconded from a community home or while staying in one has seriously disrupted the running of the home. The court is satisfied on the basis of a written report from the local authority that accommodation cannot be found in a suitable home where the young offender can stay without risk of their absconding or seriously disrupting the home.

Appeal against a remand decision

Where a juvenile court or magistrates' court dealing with a juvenile certifies that it has heard the full argument and decides on a remand to custody, the defendant may appeal to the Crown Court or High Court to consider and grant bail.

Non-custodial sentences

Supervision orders can be imposed up to the age of 17. They are similar to adult probation orders but generally a social worker will oversee instead of a probation officer. The court may include special requirements, such as a programme of specified activities, which the offender must agree to first. Supervision orders may also be combined with intermediate treatment. In addition, special restrictions can be imposed such as 'night restrictions', whereby the young offender must stay at home after dark, though this is extremely rare.

Attendance centres are run by the police, usually for a couple of hours on a Saturday afternoon. There are two types: a junior attendance centre for those aged 14–16, and a senior attendance centre for those aged 17–20.

Day centres are run by the probation service. Attendance at a day centre may form part of a supervision order or a probation order.

Community service. The minimum age for community service orders is 16. It entails working in the community in some useful, unpaid capacity. The work is done for a minimum of 40 hours and a maximum of 240 hours (120 for 16 year olds) under the supervision of the community service officer, and must be completed within 12 months of the order being made. Where offenders persistently fail to turn up they can be taken back before the courts and may receive a custodial sentence.

Fines. Courts can impose fines on juveniles in the same way as for an adult (see page 27). In addition, the courts now also have powers to impose fines on the *parents* of juveniles and young offenders.

For other non-custodial sentences see adult sentences on pages 26–80.

Custodial sentences

Detention centres and youth custody no longer exist as far as the courts are concerned (though these terms are still in popular usage). All sentences for those under 21 are now known as 'detention in a young offender institution'.

'Her Majesty's pleasure' (HMP). An offender aged under 18 (at the time of the offence) who is convicted of murder will be sentenced to be detained 'during her Majesty's pleasure in such

a place and under such circumstances as the Secretary of State may direct'. This is similar to an adult life sentence.

Young offenders convicted of one of the offences other than murder for which the maximum penalty is life may also be sentenced to HMP. In this case they will be kept in a secure unit of a local authority home or in a youth custody centre during the early part of the sentence rather than in a prison.

Custody for life. Young offenders aged between 17 and 21 who are convicted of murder (or any of the other offences for which the maximum sentence is life) may be sentenced to 'custody for life'. This is the same as a life sentence except that time will be served in a young offender institution rather than a prison if that is thought to be more appropriate.

4 Remand

When police or magistrates decide that a person suspected of having committed an offence is not to be allowed their liberty while awaiting trial or a court appearance, that person is remanded in custody and becomes an unconvicted prisoner.

Periods spent on remand may vary from a few days to a period of many months. In theory, an unconvicted prisoner has special rights and privileges and prison rules were originally made to distinguish them from convicted prisoners (including those remanded for sentence). The idea seems to have been to avoid some of the more oppressive effects of custody by giving them extra privileges. In fact, conditions for those on remand are generally worse than they are for convicted prisoners. Given that a person on remand may be completely innocent and may later be found so by the courts, it seems a strange anomaly that they often spend many months in worse conditions than a convicted prisoner.

Treatment of remand prisoners

The 1964 Prison Rules set out the following suggestions for the treatment of unconvicted prisoners:

- They should be separated from convicted persons.
- They may have the services of their own doctor or dentist.
- They may occupy privately furnished cells and be relieved of cleaning duties.
- They are not obliged to receive prison haircuts.
- They need not work.
- They are allowed a visit every day and unlimited letters.

- They may receive newspapers and other items.
- They may wear their own clothes.

Under the 1964 Prison Rules prisoners were also allowed to have food and drink and certain other items brought in, but on 1 March 1988 the privilege of having food and drink brought in was withdrawn. The change in food regulations has had a knock-on effect, and though some prisons still allow cigarettes, tobacco and toiletries to be handed in by visitors, others only allow such items to be sent by post.

In practice, most so-called 'remand privileges' are worthless, subject as they are to available resources. Local prisons (where the majority of remand prisoners are held) are so overcrowded that it is not possible to give remand prisoners a privately furnished cell. The reality is that several people are likely to be crammed into a cell designed for one or two at most, and it is not always possible to keep adults and young offenders separate.

Unconvicted prisoners have the right to refuse to work, but in fact few are given the opportunity since there is so little work available in local prisons. This means that they are more likely to be confined to their cells. A prisoner on remand who refuses work will not receive any money from the prison and may not be able, therefore, to buy toiletries and other necessary extras from the prison canteen.

Remand visits. Remand prisoners are entitled to one 15-minute visit every day (excluding Christmas Day, Boxing Day, Good Friday and – in some prisons – Sunday as well), but as remand prisoners are frequently held at prisons a long way from home, daily visits may be impracticable for partners or family. Remand prisoners are allowed up to three adult visitors per visit, but they should all get to the prison at the same time since the rule is only one visit a day. However, as local prisons find it hard to cope with large numbers of inmates receiving a visit every day, visits are likely to be subject to strict time limits, and even to be reduced in number. Children can go along and no VO is needed for either adults or children. Visits are usually held between 1.30 and 3.30 pm.

Assisted visits. Partners and close family relatives of remand prisoners who are either on low income or receive income support or family credit from the DSS can claim the cost of one visit every 28 days. This also applies to any adult who escorts the close relative of a prisoner who is unable to travel alone.

Visitors who wish to claim should obtain Form F2022 and the explanatory note F2022A from the local DSS or probation office and return it to the Assisted Prison Visits Unit 10 days before wishing to make the visit. The form is simple to fill out and expenses are paid door to door whether the visitors travel by car, motorcycle, train, bus or coach. Expenses will be paid for food on longer journeys and overnight stay accommodation can also be claimed, where necessary. Payment is now made by the Assisted Prison Visits Unit, not by local DSS offices, and will be made by Giro or travel warrant.

Money. With so many restrictions on what can be taken to remand prisoners, it is probably safest for visitors to send money which can be spent in the prison canteen. To send money use cheques or postal orders together with a letter mentioning the amount. Money sent by friends or relatives or money which the prisoner had when admitted is known as 'private cash'.

Newspapers and books. All prisoners are allowed to receive newspapers, which must be sent direct from a newsagent, but they must first make a governor's application. The allowance is one daily newspaper, one Sunday newspaper, one weekly newspaper and two periodicals. Prisoners may also receive two religious periodicals and any supplied by the chaplain. Educational or technical periodicals are allowed in addition. Books can be sent in but must be in good condition. Some prisons insist on books being given to the prison library when a prisoner leaves.

Radios. A battery-operated transistor radio is allowed as long as it only receives medium and long wave. Short-wave radios are not allowed nor are radios with a mains socket or an aerial. Batteries must be bought with private cash from the canteen and are not usually allowed to be brought in.

Letters. Unconvicted prisoners do not have to use prison stamped notepaper and can write as many letters as they wish. Two second-class letters are sent at public expense. Other letters must be paid for out of private cash. There is no limit on the number of letters that a prisoner can receive, but if letters are considered too long by prison staff they may be sent back with a slip marked 'excess mail'. All remand prisoners' letters (except to or from a legal adviser) are read by the censor as they enter or leave the prison.

Letters to legal advisers are sent at the prisoner's own expense, but the governor can allow extra letters at public expense if these are considered essential to a prisoner's defence. Prisoners should seal the envelopes themselves of all letters to legal advisers (including matters dealing with domestic or civil court cases) as these should not be read by prison officers. There is a Prison Standing Order which allows mail to and from legal advisers to pass through without being censored and such letters should be marked 'SO 5B 32 (3)' on the envelope. If prison staff wish to check a letter from a legal adviser for any reason, the letter should be opened in front of the prisoner. If staff suspect that a letter may not have come from a legal adviser they can telephone the firm to check. In general, though, letters from legal advisers should not be opened or read by prison staff.

Telephone calls. Remand prisoners are not usually allowed to make telephone calls but it is always worth asking, especially if the call is needed in order to contact a lawyer.

Clothing. Unconvicted prisoners in men's prisons can wear their own clothes providing they meet prison standards of being 'suitable, tidy and clean'. Visitors can bring in changes of clothes but those who do not receive regular visits may find it impracticable to wear their own clothes since it is difficult to wash anything more than underwear and socks in prison. Remand prisoners will be issued with a prison uniform consisting of brown jacket and trousers if they prefer or have no suitable clothes (convicted prisoners wear a grey/blue uniform).

All women prisoners, convicted or unconvicted, do not wear prison uniform and can wear their own clothes. Their clothing must be 'suitable, tidy and clean' to meet prison standards, and a female prisoner who has no suitable clothes of her own is supplied with civilian clothes by the prison.

All prisoners wear civilian clothes for court appearances. If a prisoner does not have suitable clothes of his own, the prison must supply civilian clothes for a court appearance.

Claiming benefit on remand

While you are on remand you can claim housing costs but not other benefits. If you were claiming benefits before you went to prison, it is important to write to your local DSS office as soon as possible to let them know about your new situation. If you have been claiming benefit for a partner and dependent children, they should go at once to the DSS to explain the change in circumstances so that payments will not be held up.

Housing costs benefit

You are entitled to claim housing benefit to cover your 'eligible rent' (which usually excludes fuel and hot water costs), and 80 per cent of your general rates. If previously you were claiming income support, you should let the rates department know about your situation as soon as possible as you will now be short of your rates by 20 per cent (the amount that was previously covered by your housing benefit), and you will have rate arrears facing you on your release unless you can make other arrangements for paying. If you do not inform them you may find that legal action is taken against you for rate arrears. You should also contact your landlord (if any) to discuss any shortfall of your rent which would previously have been covered by housing benefit. For further information regarding housing costs and mortgages, see page 54.

How to get advice and help

The Prison Reform Trust have produced a 'Prisoners' Information Pack' which is free to prisoners and their families. The Women Prisoners' Resource Centre have produced a 'Reception Pack' which is also free to prisoners and their families. Both packs contain detailed and comprehensive information on all aspects of prisoners' rights and potential problems. Ask the probation officer at the prison or write direct (see page 193).

There are a number of groups geared to help prisoners. Some of these will help families as well (there are other groups that exist especially to help partners and families). See pages 186–92.

For further information all prisoners should read 'Coping in prison', pages 49–66. Women prisoners should also read 'Women in prison', pages 67–78.

5 The Crown Court

Crown Courts deal with the following types of cases:
- cases which could have been heard by a magistrates' court but where the defendant has chosen to go for trial by jury at a Crown Court instead
- serious cases such as murder, manslaughter, rape or robbery
- cases which the magistrates' court have decided are too serious for them to handle
- cases where a defendant has been convicted by magistrates who have decided that the crime merits a longer sentence than they can impose
- appeals against convictions or sentences passed by the magistrates' court. In the case of an appeal against conviction, the Crown Court judge re-hears the evidence that has been given in the lower court. There is no jury present and instead the judge sits with two, three or four lay magistrates

Procedure

The procedure is similar to that of the magistrates' court except that the atmosphere is more formal. The judge, judge's clerk and barristers wear wigs and gowns. The main difference in procedure is that a jury of 12 ordinary citizens, with no specialised knowledge of the law, listen to the evidence which is presented in court and decide whether they believe the defendant to be guilty or not guilty.

There is no jury present at a Crown Court when the defendant pleads guilty, or if the case was previously tried at a magistrates' court and either the judge is passing sentence or the offender is appealing against a conviction from the magistrates' court.

As in a magistrates' court, the judge can call for various reports to help him or her to decide what type of sentence to pass. It is also open to the defence to call 'character witnesses' in favour of the accused.

The defence and prosecution each present their evidence in turn. Witnesses are 'sworn' and take the witness box to give evidence. When both sides have given their evidence the judge sums up and directs the attention of the jury to any points that he or she wishes them particularly to bear in mind. The jury are then confined to a special room where they can consider the evidence and reach a unanimous decision.

The jury retire to consider the evidence in private. If more than two hours elapse without the jury being able to reach a unanimous verdict, the judge will call them back and tell them that they may now reach a majority verdict providing at least 10 members of the jury are in agreement.

The jury then return to the court having reached either a majority or a unanimous decision. The clerk asks the jury foreman for their verdict. The jury foreman will reply either 'guilty' or 'not guilty'. If the jury have found the defendant to be 'not guilty', the defendant is released from custody.

If the defendant is found guilty by the jury the judge will call for any reports deemed necessary to help him or her decide what sentence to pass. This could be a social inquiry report (sometimes called a probation report) which will be prepared by a probation officer attached to the court. If the accused has a history of mental illness, alcoholism or drug dependency, medical reports may be called for as well. The social inquiry report will probably have been prepared during the time the prisoner was on remand and will give the court some indication of the accused's background. It may also contain a recommendation as to the sort of sentence the probation officer considers right for this particular individual.

The prosecution counsel now gives the judge details of any previous criminal record and also tells the judge whether the accused is already on probation or has been given a suspended sentence for another offence. At this stage the accused may ask, through counsel, for any similar offences they have committed to be 'taken into consideration' in order that any such offences will not be the subject of another prosecution at some future date.

The defence counsel will present a plea in mitigation putting forward any reasons why the judge should deal leniently with the accused. Any positive factors that can be produced will be brought forward at this stage.

Finally the judge pronounces sentence.

Sentencing

There are a number of non-custodial sentences that a judge can pass. These are listed on pages 26–8. If defendants are found guilty and are not given one of these 'alternatives to custody', they must go to prison. How long for and where the prisoner goes depend on the seriousness of the offence.

Receiving a custodial sentence

A custodial sentence determines a fixed period of time to be served in either one or a variety of HM prisons. Within 24 hours of being sentenced, prisoners will be given their earliest date of release (EDR) which takes into account any time spent in custody. The EDR is half the sentence for a sentence of 12 months or less (unless that leaves less than five days), or two-thirds of the sentence if it is for more than 12 months. Time spent in custody before sentence is regarded as part of the sentence. The last half (sentences of 12 months or under) or third (sentences of over 12 months) of a sentence is *remission* and this is automatically deducted from the sentence, but part or all of it can be lost for breach of prison rules or any sort of misbehaviour.

Hospital order

Under section 37 of the Mental Health Act 1983, a magistrate or judge may commit an offender to a mental hospital for any offence which might have carried a sentence of imprisonment (with the exception of murder where the fixed sentence is life). For this the evidence of two doctors who have examined the offender is needed. The evidence can be given orally or in writing.

Life sentences

There are two types of life sentence – mandatory and discretionary. Life imprisonment is the only sentence that can be passed for murder and is therefore a *mandatory* sentence for murder. Certain other offences (which could receive a sentence of a fixed term of imprisonment) can carry a life sentence if the trial judge so decides. These offences include manslaughter, armed robbery, arson, rape, kidnapping and causing an explosion. Because the judge is not bound to impose a life sentence and has a choice, a life sentence awarded in these circumstances is known as a *discretionary* life sentence.

In the case of all life sentence prisoners a tariff date is fixed soon after the trial. The trial judge will write to the Home Secretary giving his or her views and the Home Secretary will also confer with the Lord Chief Justice. The tariff date is not a release date and a life sentence prisoner, whether mandatory or discretionary, does not start the sentence with an EDR as do prisoners serving a fixed sentence. The only route to release for a lifer is through receiving a life licence from the parole board. The tariff date merely determines when the first parole review might be expected to take place and sets a minimum length of time that the offender must serve. Such things as behaviour in prison may also affect the timing of the first parole review, but no lifer will be considered for parole *before* the tariff date is reached.

In the case of discretionary lifers the judge's suggestion becomes the tariff date. This will be equivalent to the determinate sentence the judge might have passed had a life sentence not been decided upon.

Where a mandatory life sentence is imposed the trial judge and the Lord Chief Justice still write to the Home Secretary giving their views. However, the Home Secretary will have the final say and may decide to add whatever he or she considers necessary for the protection of the public.

For an offender who is under 18 at the time of the offence and is convicted of murder the sentence is not called 'life'. Instead, the offender is ordered to be detained 'during Her Majesty's pleasure' (often referred to as HMP). This is similar to a life sentence but it provides for the fact that the young prisoner may be detained 'in such a place and under such circumstances as the Secretary of State may direct'. This also applies for those under 17 who are convicted of one of the offences (other than murder) which carry a possible maximum of a life sentence. This allows for young offenders to be kept in a secure unit of a local authority home or in a young offender institution during the early part of the sentence, rather than in a prison.

Offenders between the ages of 17 and 21 who are convicted of murder (or any of the other offences for which the maximum penalty is life) may also be sentenced to custody for life. This is the same as a life sentence except that they can be kept in a young offender institution rather than a prison.

Every life sentence – mandatory, discretionary, HMP or custody for life – is an indeterminate sentence. This means that for most of the time the offender is in prison they will have only a rough idea of when they might be considered for parole and there is no guarantee of release at any pre-determined date.

After a custodial sentence is pronounced

The convicted prisoner will be taken below to the cells to await transport to the prison where the sentence will begin. A prisoner who has been sentenced can only come back to court by lodging an appeal.

Seeing a prisoner after sentence at a Crown Court

When the court has ended for the day it may be possible to see a prisoner in the cells. Ask the defence solicitor or the gaoler. The solicitor might agree to approach the gaoler for you if you find this difficult.

Appeals

Just as appeals against convictions or sentences passed by the magistrates' court can be heard by a Crown Court, appeals against conviction in the Crown Court can be taken to a judge at the Court of Appeal who will reconsider the evidence.

Appeals against conviction. The Court of Appeal exists to correct any mistakes of law that the judge may have made at the trial or to consider fresh evidence. A convicted prisoner has to apply for leave to appeal. Appeals take time to prepare and most appeals are turned down at the pre-appeal stage because they do not meet either of the above criteria.

Appeals against sentence. Prisoners who consider their sentence is too harsh, or inappropriate for the offence committed, and wish to appeal against it must do so within five days.

Appeals against lenient sentences. In 1988 the Home Secretary announced the introduction of a new procedure for appeals against over-lenient sentences to apply only to very serious cases heard at a Crown Court. The law is held to reflect public opinion and doubtless public outcry over lenient sentences for savage rape cases and other violent crimes played a part in this decision. Under the new rules, the Attorney General may, when he or she regards a sentence as too lenient, refer the case to the Court of Appeal.

Appeals to the House of Lords. The House of Lords can only consider an appeal which has first been heard by the Court of Appeal. The Court of Appeal must certify a point of law of public importance for the case to merit consideration by the House of Lords.

Part II
Prison

6 Coping in prison

After sentence has been pronounced you will usually be taken first to a local prison or remand centre to begin your sentence. If you are serving a short sentence you may stay on there until you are released. However, you may be moved to continue your sentence at a 'training' or 'dispersal' prison. If you are serving a long sentence this will just be the first step on your journey and when you move it may be the first of several such moves. For someone serving a first sentence the first few days in prison can be the hardest time of all. You must adjust to a sudden loss of liberty and the fact that everything you do from now until the time you are released is subject to regulation and control by others. You can no longer make your own decisions either about small things in your daily life or about more important matters, and you have lost the power to choose to do things on the spur of the moment. Everything has to be planned and applied for, even seeing and writing to the people closest to you. One of the first things you may want to consider is whether you wish to appeal against your sentence.

Reception

This is the process that finally makes you a part of 'the system'. In reception an officer will fill in a form about you which will follow you to any prison you might later be moved to. You will be asked your name and age and what sentence you are serving, whether you have any distinguishing marks and what your religion is. You will hand over your clothes and private property and in their place be given a uniform and a prison number. That prison number will remain the same throughout your sentence and through any number of moves to different prisons, it must head your letters and be written on the envelope of all incoming letters. You will also be given a reception letter to let people know where you are. You should be asked if you wish to appeal against your sentence. If you say that you do the legal officer should visit you to discuss this.

When you leave reception you will be allocated to a cell. A card on the door gives your name, number and religion and also what sentence you are serving. On the next working day you will have interviews or be seen by a reception board and allocated some kind of work. You will also receive a security category and this will determine the type of prison where you will serve your sentence. For those serving a long sentence, particularly a 'life' sentence, the process of induction may be carried out in greater detail and take more time.

Categorisation of prisoners

Every prisoner is classified for security reasons and given a category from A to D, A denoting the highest security risk and the highest security classification. When deciding what category to give a prisoner the authorities consider the type of offence together with the likelihood of an escape attempt and whether that particular prisoner might be a danger to the community if they did escape. The classification or categorisation of prisoners should not be confused with the way prisons are classified. Unlike your prison number, your category need not remain the same throughout your sentence. Categorisation is reviewed from time to time though there is no appeal procedure. The only thing a prisoner who thinks he has been wrongly categorised can do is to petition the Home Secretary. If you are serving a long sentence you may go down the categorisation ladder as the time approaches for your release.

Category A is for offenders 'whose escape would be highly dangerous to the public or police or the security of the state'. Category A prisoners go to maximum security prisons or to special secure wings in other prisons.

Category B is for prisoners for whom the very highest conditions of security are not necessary but for whom escape must be made very difficult. They are usually placed in 'closed' prisons where there is reasonable freedom of movement within secure conditions.

Category C prisoners are those who cannot be trusted in open conditions and for whom escape must be made very difficult. Category C offenders are allowed a high degree of unsupervised movement around the prison. They may be housed in dormitory type accommodation in prisons where often the only outer security may be a high wire fence.

Category D prisoners generally go to open prisons, but some go to other prisons as orderlies, gardeners, etc. This category may also denote a prisoner at the end of a long sentence or a 'lifer' being considered for parole.

Categorisation affects the conditions you will be held in. Category A prisoners have extra security restrictions placed on them which can also affect visiting. Their visitors must first be 'vetted' by the police and they may have to sit at certain specified tables in the visiting room.

Rule 43

Any prisoner, whatever their categorisation, may be segregated from other inmates under Prison Rule 43. This is usually done because the governor decides it is necessary for the prisoner's own protection. The reason might be that the offence is the kind that other inmates generally disapprove of. The wording of Rule 43 states that the prisoner is segregated 'for reasons of good order and discipline' or for their 'own protection'. Sometimes prisoners themselves request to go on Rule 43 for a variety of reasons. This should not be done lightly since it can be easier to go on 43 than come off it later; other prisoners may interpret a desire for seclusion as meaning there is something to hide even though this may not be the case.

Categorisation of prisons

The primary function of a penal establishment is to hold prisoners in secure conditions where they are unlikely to be able to escape. Provisions for containment vary widely and are subject to the governors' discretion. Each prison is given a security category to denote how secure it is judged to be.

Technically prisons are either 'local' or 'training'. Some types of training prisons are described as 'dispersal'. The term 'dispersal' arose first some years ago when a study was done as to whether it was better to put all potentially violent or dangerous prisoners into one sort of prison and those who had committed lesser crimes into another. It was decided that it was better to create a 'mix' and to disperse prisoners with the highest security rating to a variety of different prisons throughout England and Wales, hence the 'dispersal' system.

Prison categorisation should not be confused with the categorisation of inmates. It is possible for prisoners of Categories B, C and D to be held in prisons designated Category A, B or C.

Closed, maximum security and dispersal prisons

These prisons hold offenders who have been assessed as needing to be held in the most secure conditions. However, some Category A prisoners are held in special security units in 'local prisons'. A 'training' prison will have opportunities for acquiring work skills which should be useful after release.

Security is based on a combination of four factors: a secure outer perimeter, locks and keys, bars, and visual checks. High security prisons may vary widely in the security aids in force. More modern high security prisons may have searchlights, closed-circuit TV and electrically controlled gates and doors. Older prisons, built before 1955, usually have a gatehouse separated from the main block of the prison by a courtyard. There may also be guard dogs.

Local prisons

These are prisons where offenders are either serving short sentences or passing through or on remand, with the exception of those which have special high-security wings to hold prisoners with a high-security rating. There is likely to be little chance for training or education and there is likely to be overcrowding and a lack of the type of facilities afforded by training or dispersal prisons generally.

Semi-open prisons

A semi-open prison combines some of the factors of a maximum security prison with other features more common to an open prison. Each prison, however, is under the command of a prison governor and individual variations are at the governor's discretion.

Open prisons

In open prisons the responsibility rests on the inmate to abide by the rules and the primary rule is not to abscond. Prisoners are not likely to be assessed as suitable for open prisons until or unless they are judged to be likely to abide by this rule. Security usually amounts to no more than a wire fence around the perimeter. The function of an open prison is to acclimatise inmates gradually to the outside world. Usually they will have opportunities to go in and out of the prison for education or leisure activities. In the latter part of their sentence they may also be allowed to 'work out'. Within the outer perimeter of the prison inmates have almost total freedom to go wherever they wish, except for any areas designated as being out of bounds to prisoners.

Allocation to a particular prison

Allocation depends on length of sentence, security categorisation and where space is available at the time. Unless you are serving a short sentence you will usually be allocated to a training prison. Young offenders (under 21) will be moved to a young offender institution soon after sentence. The prison you go to may be a long way from where you live. If you want to apply to be sent to a prison nearer home and have a good reason, such as the illness of a close relative or because your partner is in an advanced state of pregnancy, you should ask to see the governor as soon as possible and tell him about your situation, or you could speak to the officer in charge of allocation. You may need a letter from a doctor, probation officer or social worker to support your request and prove that you are telling the truth.

For allocation of lifers, young offenders serving HMP or custody for life, see page 81.

Appeals against sentence and conviction

If you said at reception that you did not wish to appeal against your sentence and have changed your mind, ask to see the legal officer as soon as possible. You must do this within eight days of starting your sentence.

For appeals against conviction there must either be fresh evidence that was not available at the time of your trial or else

the trial must have been wrongly conducted in some way. Your
solicitor will be able to advise you in either case.

Entitlement to benefits

If you were claiming benefit before you went to prison you
should write to your local DSS office to let them know what is
happening. The only benefit you can claim while in prison is to
cover housing costs. If you have been claiming benefit for a
partner and dependent children, your partner should go to the
DSS as quickly as possible to explain the change of
circumstances. It is important to do this at once to avoid delay
in payment. Depending on your circumstances you may be able
to claim housing costs while you are in prison.

Tenants (council or private)

If you are serving a sentence of one year (52 weeks) or less you
can draw housing benefit to help you keep it on. You should
also receive 80 per cent of your rates (excluding water rates)
unless you have savings of more than £8,000. (If you have
savings of over £3,000 your housing benefit will be reduced.)
Get in touch with:

- the housing benefit office and the DSS. If you are already
  claiming benefit tell the benefit office of your changed
  circumstances and say you wish to go on claiming. If not
  write to your local council and ask for a housing benefit
  form.
- your landlord (council or private). Explain your changed
  circumstances and say that you are making arrangements to
  have housing costs paid direct to them.
- your insurers (if any). Let them know you will be away
  from the property for a time.

Buying your own home

Get in touch with your bank or building society and explain the
situation. You may be able to have payments frozen. If you are
forced to sell your home they may be able to arrange the sale
for you. Also get in touch with the local council to ask for
housing benefit. You may be able to claim up to 80 per cent of
your general rates but no water rates. Ask them to send you a
housing benefit form.

Life in prison

Letters

Letters can only be written on special double sheets of prison notepaper as supplied by the Prison Department. These blue-lined sheets of paper, stamped at the top with the address of the prison, are always called 'letters' and an envelope is supplied with each one. Each prisoner is entitled to one free letter and stamp every week and in addition to this statutory allowance may also buy an extra letter and stamp every week from the canteen. In long-term prisons inmates may be allowed to buy more extra letters but this varies from prison to prison.

Canteen

The prison canteen is a small shop where prisoners can spend prison earnings (and in some cases private cash) on tobacco, sweets, biscuits, toiletries and radio batteries. Extra stamps can only be purchased with prison earnings.

Receiving money from outside

Prisoners are allowed to receive some private cash from outside to pay for canteen items, newspapers ordered from a newsagent or books sent away for. Money should always be sent in the form of a postal order or by registered post or recorded delivery. A letter should always be enclosed mentioning the sum sent. Mail can go astray in prison.

Health

Your medical care is now the responsibility of the prison medical service, which is not part of the NHS. Routine medical care is provided by prison officers who have done a short training course. (In women's prisons qualified nurses are employed.) Notify the prison medical officer on reception if you have been having any regular medication and if you are allergic to any form of medication. Your previous medical records do not normally follow you into prison if your sentence is for less than two years. As a convicted prisoner you cannot ask for a second opinion. Dental and optical services are available to prisoners on longer sentences or in urgent need and you will not usually have to pay.

The right to refuse medical treatment

With the exception of your medical examination at reception, you are within your rights to accept or decline medical treatment under standing order 13, and this includes psychiatric treatment. However, the rule has a 'get-out' clause that you must not be 'incapable of forming a rational decision'. This is difficult to prove. If you feel that you have a good case and that you are being given treatment or drugs that are wrong for you, contact one of the advice agencies that help prisoners (see pages 186-92).

AIDS

Aids is caused by a virus called HIV. You cannot catch HIV through normal daily contact with someone who has it. There is no risk from shaking hands, using the same plates and cutlery, the same wash basin, bath or toilet. HIV is passed on through bodily fluids such as semen or by injection of contaminated blood or by injecting yourself with a needle that has been used by someone who has HIV. No drug user, in or out of prison, should ever share a needle with anyone else, nor should they have unprotected sex (sex without using a condom). Anyone who is worried about AIDS or who wants further information should contact the Terence Higgins Trust (see page 180).

Exercise

All prisoners in closed prisons should have regular exercise periods, weather permitting. Open prisons do not have exercise periods as you can walk around more freely. You can ask to be excused from exercise on medical grounds.

Education

The only prisoners with a clearly defined right to receive education are those under school-leaving age in young offender institutions. However, there should be some educational facilities in most prisons. If you have missed out on education at school for one reason or another, this might be the time to try to catch up. Classes can cover a wide range of subjects from basic reading and writing, usually called 'Adult Literacy Schemes' to 'writer in residence' creative writing courses at some prisons. There may also be painting or other creative courses which can give a lot of satisfaction. Sometimes people who have never even held a paintbrush before start to paint in prison and discover a talent they never knew they had. Adult prisoners can apply to go on full-time education but there is often a waiting list. If you fancy having a go at higher education there are Open University courses available in some long-term prisons, and if you are really keen you can always make a governors' application for re-allocation to a prison where such courses are available. Prison authorities are generally keen to encourage anyone who shows a real desire to better themselves in this way.

Personal problems

The problems you face in prison may range from practical day-to-day difficulties to a major crisis over a relationship. The prison probation officer or social worker within the prison should be your first port of call. Or, if you are already in touch with a probation officer outside, you should be able to write and receive letters from him or her and may be able to have a visit. Prison probation officers used to be known as welfare officers and some prisoners and prison officers still refer to them as 'the welfare'. Another port of call may be the prison chaplain. Many prison officers today like to be involved in the welfare of prisoners instead of just being seen as 'turnkeys'. It is difficult to generalise about this because in the end it is down to the individuals concerned, but when a prisoner has a good relationship with his or her 'landing' or 'wing' officer this may be a good place to begin to sort out personal problems or difficulties. Or you may decide to have visits from a VA (voluntary associate) or prison visitor (see pages 58–60). If you have a problem connected with your partner or with family matters you might want to ask for a 'special visit' or a 'welfare' visit.

Special or welfare visits, accumulated visits

Normally, visits are allowed every 28 days, although in long-term prisons visits are usually more frequent and may be allowed every fortnight. If you have a good reason for needing an extra visit to discuss family matters you should apply to the governor for a 'special visit', or 'welfare visit' as these are sometimes called. If the governor thinks the reason is good enough the request will normally be granted. The probation officer at the prison may also be able to arrange a special visit, which will either take place in one of the welfare offices or the visiting room. Usually they will be supervised by the probation officer instead of prison officers. When a prisoner is at a prison a long way from home and a partner or relative is finding it difficult to make the journey very often, visits can sometimes be arranged close together on consecutive days. These are known as 'accumulated visits'. Make an application if you want to have your visits this way. Sometimes a prisoner can 'save up' visits and be moved to a prison nearer home for a time so family and friends can visit there. Some prisons have a nearby hostel where partners or family can stay at low cost. This makes visiting easier for people who have a long way to travel. Ask the probation officer or see the Prison Visiting Chart, pages 124–173.

Keeping contact with the outside world

If there is no one to visit you because you have lost touch with your family or are divorced, you may start to feel very isolated. If so talk to the prison probation officer about the possibility of having a VA (voluntary associate). These volunteers befriend prisoners and aim to help break up the monotony of prison life through visits and letters. VAs are independent of the prison and the Home Office and are not to be confused with prison visitors.

Who are VAs and why might I want one to visit me?

VAs are ordinary people from all walks of life. They can be teachers, lawyers or professionals of some other kind or they can be ex-prisoners, housewives, students, retired people or ordinary working people in any kind of job. All VAs must satisfy the people in charge of their group that they will be able to make friends easily with someone in prison and understand their problems. Usually the person in charge of the group will try to match people of similar interests.

A VA can be male or female, old or young and of any colour, race or creed. They are not paid, although they should get their visiting expenses. There are two types of VAs. Some VAs are attached to the local probation service and your probation officer at the prison will be able to tell you if there is a group locally and put you in touch with them. There is also an independent group called New Bridge. If you want a New Bridge VA you can either write direct to them or ask the probation officer to make the first approach for you.

New Bridge VAs

Though the New Bridge office is in London, their VAs are not restricted to visiting prisons in or near London and will visit prisons over a wide area, whereas local probation group VAs only visit in or near their own area. New Bridge have their own system of working. The way it usually works is that, having first decided they want a VA, the offender agrees to having details sent to New Bridge by the probation officer. The details will include the type of offence, the sentence, a list of previous convictions and whether the offender has any particular interests. This information helps New Bridge to allocate a suitable VA. Such information is, of course, privileged and confidential and must not be discussed outside that particular group, even with other New Bridge members. VAs are divided into groups, each having its own chairman or group leader. The group leader will try to allocate the case to the VA who seems most suitable. Any inmate can apply, regardless of the offence committed, and no offence bars any offender from having a VA. However, no VA is forced to take on a particular case since it is clearly in the interests of both parties that the two should be able to get on with one another and enjoy some common interests as well if possible.

The VA will then write to the offender introducing themselves. Some prisoners prefer to just write and receive letters but most want a visit once the ice has been broken. When you and your VA agree to have a visit you send a VO just as you would for any other visitor.

A VA visits in the visiting room like any other visitor, unlike a prison visitor. Other inmates need never know your visitor is a VA if you don't want them to and some prisoners prefer to keep this private.

When the time comes for release your VA will generally be on hand to help with practical problems as well as being a supportive friend. However, this is between the two people concerned and some offenders prefer to leave behind everything that reminds them of prison – even good friends. If you are interested in having a New Bridge VA, discuss it with the probation officer or write direct to New Bridge (see page 189).

Probation VAs

In many parts of the country groups of local people work as VAs with the local probation service. One voluntary group, called Catholic Social Service for Prisoners, have been visiting prisoners since 1898. Their volunteers visit about 200 prisoners a year through the probation officer or the chaplain. They will visit offenders of any religion or none so do not let the name put you off if you are not a Catholic. They offer two types of service: counselling, practical help and advice for those serving short terms or who have just been admitted; and long-term support and counselling for those serving very long sentences or doing life.

Talk to the prison probation officer about having a VA or write direct to the Catholic Social Service for Prisoners if you prefer (see page 187).

Prison visitors

In some prisons local people, who have first been approved by the Home Office, visit prisoners for a friendly chat. They are not the same as VAs and do not visit in the visiting room like ordinary visitors. If the offender is moved to another prison the visits cease, and the prisoner will have to ask for a new prison visitor at the new prison. The friendship ends once the prisoner is released. Speak to the chaplain if you are interested in having a prison visitor.

Books and newspapers

All prisoners can have newspapers but the rule is that they must be sent direct from a newsagent. Some long-term or open prisons may be more relaxed about this rule and allow your visitors to bring in a week's supply of papers that have already been read. This can be a help when money is tight. You can order them yourself or someone outside can do this for you. The allowance is one daily newspaper, one Sunday and one weekly newspaper as well as two periodicals and two religious periodicals and any supplied by the chaplain. Prisoners should be allowed educational or technical periodicals in addition.

The rule about books in most prisons is that they have to be sent in and cannot be handed over as property on a visit, but again this does vary from prison to prison and it's best to check. Books should be in good condition. If you ask a visitor to get you expensive hobby books bear in mind that some prisons insist on books being left in the prison library when a prisoner leaves. The prison library should be able to get books for you from the local council library. You should also be able to see a copy of the Prison Rules on open display in the library as well as Prison Standing Orders 3C, 4, 5 and 12, European Prison Rules and documents giving advice on making petitions and on parole.

Radios

Radios are allowed in most prisons. The radio should be battery operated and without an aerial or mains socket. It must only be capable of receiving medium and short wave. Long-wave radio sets are not allowed in any prison. Batteries usually have to be bought from the canteen but this does vary from prison to prison.

Using the telephone

Sentenced prisoners in all open and Category C prisons, and other prisons as authorised by the Home Secretary, can now make telephone calls. Phone cards from prison canteens are allowed up to an amount of £4 a month. Remand prisoners are not normally allowed to make telephone calls and visitors cannot ring prisoners.

Practising your religion

You have a right to practise your religion while you are in prison as long as it is one which the Prison Department recognise. You will be asked your religion at reception and it will be noted on your cell card. Every prison has at least one Church of England chaplain attached to the prison, either full or part time. Ministers of other religions and other denominations visit the prison regularly, but if no one from your religion is visiting regularly, talk to the prison chaplain who should be able to help.

The Home Office have produced a *Directory and Guide on Religious Practices in HM Prison Service* to assist officers in seeing that every prisoner shall be able to observe recognised religious practices. The guide covers Buddhism, Hinduism, Islam, Judiasm and Sikkism. Part II (available in autumn 1989) will cover Baha'i, Church of Jesus Christ of Latter Day Saints (Mormon), Jainism and Rastafarianism. However, the Home Office say that the inclusion of Rastafarianism is subject to the various groups being able to agree on a common article of faith and to recognise a common religious leader in time for final preparation of Part II. They say that they are committed to the policy that any person shall be allowed to practise his or her religion while in prison and that 'culturally' they have acknowledged Rastafarianism, they do not cut off dreadlocks and do allow colours and wristbands to be worn.

The Rastafarian Advisory Centre say that Rastafarianism is not recognised as a religion by the prison service and that they find it difficult, therefore, to follow their faith and observe correct dietary laws. Of course, any prisoner with individual problems can always apply to see the governor. Rastafarians with problems or who wish to know more about the current situation in prison can contact the Rastafarian Advisory Centre. (See page 191).

Special diets

Prisoners should, in theory, be able to have special diets on religious, medical or conscience grounds. Vegans may be asked for proof (such as a statement from the Vegan Society). Vegetarians should be provided with suitable meals, though how easy it is to be a vegetarian in prison may vary according to the establishment. Bear in mind that being a vegetarian outside is not easy if you have to eat out a lot. Even with a choice of restaurants it can be difficult to be a vegetarian and have a sufficiently varied and adequate diet. Jewish, Muslim, Hindu, Buddhist or Sikh prisoners should be provided with special diets. However, strictly orthodox Jews who can only eat kosher meat or Muslims who should only eat Halal meat may, temporarily, have to become vegetarians. The same may apply to Rastafarians. This will obviously vary from prison to prison and the Home Office say that their policy is to make every effort to provide special diets. Where large groups of one kind of religious or other group are concentrated this will obviously be easier than if there are only one or two.

Ethnic minority groups

There is statistical evidence that black people suffer higher arrest rates, harsher sentencing and are also likely to have a standard of treatment in prison which is below that of their white counterparts. Although black people make up only just over 4 per cent of the population in the UK, the percentage of black prisoners has risen from 12.5 per cent in 1985 to 14 per cent in 1987. The most recent NACRO report estimates that 'nearly one in ten young men in the black community will have been locked up by his 21st birthday'. Add to this a recent Home Office survey which concluded that 'more whites hold desirable jobs (inside) and more non-whites are being punished', and it is clear that with prisons under stress anyway due to overcrowding, the situation is bound to lead to some resentment and anger among the prison population. However, the Home Office say that they are committed absolutely to a policy of racial equality and in November 1986 they issued the following Race Relations Policy Statement on behalf of HM Prison Service:

1   The Prison Department is committed absolutely to a policy of racial equality and to the elimination of discrimination in all aspects of the work of the Prison Service. It is opposed also to any display of racial prejudice, either by word or conduct by any member of the Service in his or her dealings with any other person.
2   All prisoners should be treated with humanity and respect. All prisoners should be treated impartially and without discrimination on grounds of colour, race or religion. Insulting, abusive or derogatory language towards prisoners will not be tolerated.
3   Race relations concern every member of the Prison Service. It is the responsibility of every member of staff to ensure that the Department's policy is carried out in relation to other members of staff as well as prisoners.
4   Members of minority religious groups have the same right to practise their faith as those of the majority faith. Wherever feasible in prison circumstances arrangements are made to give them the same practical opportunity to do so.
5   All inmates should have equal access to the facilities provided in the establishment including jobs. The distribution of inmates throughout the establishment and its facilities should as far as is practicable and sensible be broadly responsive to the ethnic mix of the establishment.
6   No particular racial group should be allowed to dominate any activity to the unfair exclusion of others.

There is now a race relations co-ordinator in every region and every prison now has a race relations liaison officer (likely to be of governor grade), whose job it is to deal with all matters relating to race relations, including complaints. There is also a race relations committee which includes a chaplain and two others. It is the responsibility of the governor of every prison to make sure that race relations within the prison are harmonious.

Any black prisoner who encounters racial discrimination of any kind in prison should refer to the above policy statement. A number of ethnic minorities now have their own self-help and voluntary groups who will visit and befriend offenders or help their families. However, any support group for prisoners or families will be pleased to help you if they can and refer you elsewhere if they cannot. Most voluntary groups try to recruit volunteers of every race, colour and creed. For details of all groups see pages 186–92.

Punishment

By the Board of Visitors

Punishments are known as 'awards' in the prison disciplinary system. The prison governor handles minor incidents and all serious breaches of discipline are dealt with by a prison's Board of Visitors. Members of the Board of Visitors are drawn from the local community and are appointed personally by the Home Secretary. Many are magistrates. The boards have a dual role because they also act as watchdog to hear complaints and requests from prisoners. The punishments they can award are a caution, cellular confinement and loss of privileges for a period of any length. They can also exclude prisoners from associated work for up to 56 days, stop earnings for up to 36 days and order loss of remission for up to 180 days.

There is no provision for legal representation at governors' hearings, though it is technically possible to be represented at Board of Visitors' hearings allowing for a number of factors such as the seriousness of the charge and the potential penalty. However, it is rare for prisoners to bother. The *Manual on the Conduct of Adjudications* is available in the prison library and should be on open display. In some prisons it seems you have to ask for it. It might be worth asking to see it even if you are segregated pending your adjudication and cannot get to the library. If you are not given the chance to see it you could request that the adjudication be adjourned until you are able to consult it. Instead of legal representation you may be allowed to have the help of a friend or adviser. Such an adviser is usually called a 'McKenzie man' and might be another prisoner, a prison officer, a probation officer or the chaplain. The 'McKenzie man' is simply there to take notes and give advice and cannot speak at the adjudication without the board's permission.

Informal punishments

In addition to the formal disciplinary system there are other punishments the prison can use without holding a disciplinary hearing. Prisoners' property can be confiscated or they may be segregated from other prisoners. There are other less obvious ways of punishing prisoners, more difficult to challenge, such as giving a change of categorisation or an unfavourable parole report. A change of work may be given or an inmate placed on Rule 43. A prisoner who thinks he or she has been unfairly treated can apply to the Board of Visitors, petition the Home Secretary or make an application to see the Home Secretary's visiting officer. However, such practices have never been successfully challenged in the courts and the Home Office regards them merely as matters of 'administration'.

Being 'ghosted'

Sometimes prisoners are moved suddenly without warning. This is not a normal scheduled move. A prisoner will be told he is being moved only hours at most before the move takes place. Prisoners are 'ghosted' because there is some reason why the authorities want to move that inmate away from the particular prison. It's a 'now you see me, now you don't' situation. If you are 'ghosted' just before a visit you may be concerned about letting your partner or family know that you've gone. A probation officer or sympathetic 'landing' or 'wing' officer might be able to help either before or after you're moved.

Being 'in patches'

A male prisoner who has made an escape attempt has to wear special prison clothing which has distinctive patches sewn on, usually yellow, so that he will be clearly visible should he be tempted to make another such attempt.

Further information

For more information on all aspects of prison life ask the probation officer or the chaplain for the 'Prisoners Information Pack' produced by the Prison Reform Trust. If you prefer you can write direct to the Trust. For women prisoners, the Women Prisoners' Resource Centre have produced a 'Reception Pack'.

You can obtain one of these in the same way, through the prison probation officer or chaplain or by writing direct. Both are free to prisoners and their families, and contain much detailed and useful information (see page 193).

7 Women in prison and children in care

Do women get a raw deal from the criminal justice system?

Women who go to prison – just as many women outside prison walls – face additional problems simply because they are women. The reasons are complex.

Men in the armed forces, police and other uniformed services outnumber women by a very high ratio. It would seem, therefore, that on the whole men are more often attracted to a single-sex environment with an accent on discipline and conformity than women are. The prison system is based on just such a male ethic and consequently it is alien to most women, who find it harder than men to cope, possibly without even knowing why. Indeed, this is officially recognised in that women no longer have to wear prison uniform. There is less recognition, however, of the greater psychological damage that prison inflicts on a woman, for whom a custodial sentence contains a hidden punishment in the inevitable erosion of her femininity and consequent lowering of self-image, whereas (leaving social stigma aside) it does nothing to destroy a man's masculinity. On the contrary, most people regard men who go to prison as having a 'macho' image.

Imprisonment for petty offences

The vast majority of women who receive a custodial sentence are convicted of a minor offence against property or some other minor and non-violent offence. A very large proportion are sent to prison because they are given a fine that they cannot afford to pay. Alternatives to a prison sentence (including the option of community service) are statistically less likely to be offered to women than men. So while it is true that a smaller proportion of women overall than men get custodial sentences, it is a sobering fact that the total number of women sentenced to prison has increased threefold since 1974, from 800 to 2,400. This means that while fewer women get custodial sentences overall, the percentage is increasing substantially faster than it is for men. (These statistics are taken from a report produced by the Women's Equality Group of the London Strategic Policy Unit. Copies can be obtained from NACRO. See page 193.)

Treatment in prison and additional problems faced by women

The regime in women's prisons is more rigid and the discipline harsher: women prisoners are more than twice as likely to be disciplined as men. In what seems to be a hangover from Victorian values, the treatment of women in prison still seems to reflect the view that their problems spring largely from failure in the traditional feminine role of homemaker, wife and mother and can be solved if they learn to make a success of their lives as women. So where in men's prisons the emphasis is on training for a trade and preparing for release, for women the accent still seems to be on learning homemaking and child-care, even though they may well have no supportive male figure around. Though clearly such skills are useful for anyone who has been institutionalised (men as well as women), the reality is that many women come out to face financial stress. The female ex-offender, who may have children as well as herself to support, is likely to have as many problems relating to her inability to achieve economic independence as that of any male ex-offender.

There is also a greater use of drug treatment for women in prison. In the world outside women are more likely than men to seek the help of a doctor. According to a recent report by the House of Commons social services committee on the prison medical service, women prisoners pose a particular problem for this reason in spite of their relatively small numbers. The prison medical association claims that 'women inmates include the most disturbed women in the population outside of the special hospitals', but they also admit that the extra stress placed on women by the prison environment seems to cause women 'to suffer more than men from the emotional strain of imprison-ment and separation from their families'.

The result of this extra stress is that the rate at which drugs are dispensed to women prisoners is significantly higher than for male prisoners. In particular, the level of psychotropic drugs administered is very high indeed. There are also numbers of women in prison who the prison medical officers believe should not be in prison at all but detained in hospital under the Mental Health Act 1983.

The location of prisons causes additional problems for women. The equation of more men than women in prison results in fewer penal establishments for women, who are therefore more likely than men to be sent to a prison distant from their home. This results in fewer visits and a greater likelihood of isolation from family or friends.

Rehabilitation

Women, in general, have less contact with the probation service, probably because they tend to commit a range of lesser offences carrying shorter sentences, even though overall they serve longer sentences than men for the same offences. Being less used to probation officers, women ex-offenders are less likely to turn to them for help. Black women ex-offenders are even further disadvantaged in this respect since they perceive the probation service as being largely composed of white males. In fact, in the Inner London area there are more women than men probation officers at basic grade but they are largely white. Although efforts are being made to recruit more black probation officers, the lack of black people in the probation service is still a problem. Drug and alcohol projects, geared to male ex-offenders, are less available to women even though they are just as likely to have alcohol and drug-related problems. There are also fewer drop-in centres for women with children. The lack of provision for drug-misusers and alcohol dependents is not related to the needs of women ex-prisoners, but is nevertheless a reality.

Women prisoners and their children

Women still remain primarily responsible for child care, and when a woman is sent to prison the problem of who is to care for her children while she is away is a very real one.

When a woman is arrested and taken into custody she runs the risk of having her children put into care unless there is a supportive father or relative around. However, when suitable friends or relatives can make arrangements to take the children, social services are generally helpful and can make payments to carers.

A single-parent mother who is charged with an offence runs an even greater risk of losing care of her children even before she is taken into custody, although again, this will greatly depend on the level of support available from family or friends. All too often, however, children become innocent victims in a cycle of poverty and deprivation.

Life in prison

Most of what is said in the chapters on 'Coping in prison' (pages 49–65) and 'Remand' (pages 36–40) applies to both men and women, but there are some differences which are described below.

Clothes. You can wear your own clothes as long as the prison thinks they are suitable. If you have not got enough of your own you can get clothes from the prison. You are only allowed a limited number of garments at any one time and you should be able to use a washing machine to keep them clean. Clothes can be exchanged on visits or swapped with clothes handed over with your private property in reception.

Hair. You do not have to have your hair cut unless the medical officer makes an order stating why this is necessary. The order then has to be approved by the governor.

Toiletries. These can be bought from the canteen. Skin and hair care products for black women are not always available but you should be able to order what you need. If not, apply to see the governor.

Sanitary protection. According to Prison Standing Order 14 you should be provided with a sufficient supply of sanitary towels or tampons at the time needed. You should also be given paper to wrap used towels which should be incinerated without delay. According to the same Standing Order you should be able to ask for a supply of warm water in the evenings.

Visits. The entitlement is one 30-minute visit every 28 days for women and one every 14 days for girls under 21. Most women's prisons seem to allow visits every 14 days but your visitors will still be only able to claim the cost of one visit every 28 days from the DSS.

Location of women's prisons

There are only 12 prison department establishments for women and girls:

Closed prisons. Risley (Cheshire), Pucklechurch (near Bristol) and Low Newton (near Durham) only take women or girls who are either on remand or waiting to be allocated after sentence. Holloway (London) takes remand prisoners but also takes sentenced prisoners as well. It is supposed to provide a national centre for treating women with psychiatric problems, though this unit is to be rebuilt. New Hall (near Wakefield) takes remand prisoners and women serving short sentences. Styal (Cheshire), Cookham Wood (Kent) and Bullwood Hall (Essex) are all closed prisons for sentenced women prisoners. Cookham Wood takes only adult women, but Bullwood and Styal have a mixture of adult and young offender prisoners. Durham prison (for men) also has a closed wing (H wing) for women which takes up to 40 prisoners in high security conditions. All women and girls who are serving life or HMP start off in Durham as well as any woman who is classified as Category A (see page 50).

Open prisons. Askham Grange (near York), Drake Hall (Staffordshire) and East Sutton Park (near Maidstone, Kent) take women and girls. See page 53 for details about open prisons.

Women serving short sentences are liable to remain at remand centres for their entire sentence.

Having a baby in prison

Prison rules specify that 'The Secretary of State may, subject to any conditions he thinks fit, permit a woman prisoner to have her baby with her in prison, and everything necessary for the baby's maintenance may be provided there.'

If you are pregnant and likely to have a baby while in prison, or have recently given birth to a baby, you may be able to go to one of the three mother and baby units at Holloway, Styal or Askham Grange. Usually you will be taken to hospital for antenatal care and also to have your baby. You will return to prison after the birth.

Arrangements for pregnant women

Pregnant women prisoners should not be left alone at night so that there are others around to give help if necessary. If you refuse to share you will be asked to sign a form saying that you have asked to be on your own and know this means help will not be so easily available. In this case you should have a call bell in your cell.

If you commit a prison discipline offence while pregnant you will probably not be punished by being segregated. If you are you should still be able to share a room at night and spend the days in the segregation unit.

Mother and baby units

You can apply to the governor to have your baby with you in prison. A mother can keep her baby with her until the age of nine months at Holloway and Styal. At Askham Grange prison, which is open, babies can generally stay with their mothers up to the age of 18 months to two years. However, it is by no means automatic for a mother to have her baby with her in prison.

Whether you will be considered for a place in a mother and baby unit depends on the following:

- if you start off in a closed prison, whether the baby will be nine months old before you are either released or allowed to go to an open prison
- if you are at an open prison, whether the baby will be 18 months old before your EDR (this will not be affected by the possibility of an earlier release on parole)
- whether you are likely to look after the baby after your release. If you have other children and all were in care before you went to prison, that may count against you
- if you are suffering from a mental or physical illness which could affect your ability to look after your baby
- if you are considered 'a disruptive influence' who might not co-operate with the smooth running of the unit

Whether you will be allowed to have your baby with you or not also depends on if there is a place for you in a unit suitable to the circumstances of your sentence and security category. There are altogether 34 places in mother and baby units: 7 places at Holloway and 12 at Styal for babies under nine months, and 15 places at Askham Grange for babies under 18 months old.

The routine at mother and baby units varies but there will almost certainly be rules about when you can bath your baby and about not having the baby in your bed. Babies usually stay in the nursery for about four hours a day while you are at work or doing classes.

You can be disciplined for breaking rules like any other prisoner or even placed in a segregation unit (away from your baby) for up to 28 days. However, you should not be prevented from seeing your baby regularly and feeding him or her as well if this is practicable.

However, if it is decided to move you to another prison because of your behaviour, this could mean separation from your baby. If you were at Askham Grange, for instance, and had a baby of 12 months old, and it was decided to move you to Holloway or Styal, neither of those units would accept a baby of that age.

Early separation from your baby

If you are unable to keep your baby with you or decide not to you will usually be separated from each other within the first four weeks (at the end of four weeks if you are breast-feeding). If the prison governor thinks this will lead to serious hardship he or she can apply to the Home Office. This applies equally to convicted women and women on remand.

Visits with children

Children who are not in prison with you but living with their father or with friends or relatives can be brought for visits once a fortnight (daily if you are on remand) (see page 95 for details of 'Assisted prison visits').

If your children are in care the local authority can arrange for them to be brought to see you in prison or sometimes for you to be taken out to visit them. The local authority has to make some arrangement for you to see your children. If it does not do so you must be served with a notice. If this happens you can apply to the court to see your child.

Placing children in care

Once children have been placed in care it can be difficult to get them back. Even when a child is placed in voluntary care there is no absolute guarantee that parents will be able to get their child back. It is therefore very important for all parents (single or otherwise) to understand the legal position and what can happen. It helps to know what steps the social services and courts may take in certain situations.

NACRO have produced a leaflet which covers all aspects of placing your children in care. You can obtain this leaflet, called 'Children', from the prison probation department or direct from NACRO (see page 193). If your child is at risk of going into care you need to get expert and specialised legal advice from a solicitor who is experienced in child-care cases. (See page 181).

Local authority care

Local authorities can provide direct financial or other help such as offering a place in a nursery or a childminding place. This type of assistance is called Section 1 Help (under the Child Care Act 1980). When a parent receives a prison sentence, and relatives or friends have agreed to look after children to prevent them going into care, the local authority should be asked if they will help. They do not have to but often will if asked.

Voluntary care

If there is no one who can look after your children while you are in prison and you have to put them into voluntary care, you should try to get a clear written agreement with the local authority about the return of your child. Although parents do still have rights (the legal term is 'parental rights'), the local authority will often make major decisions about what is to happen to your children. The only way out of this difficulty may be to take them out of care. This may not be possible if you are still in prison. Once children have been in voluntary care for longer than six months you must give 28 days' notice if you want to take over their care again. If the local authority does not want to return your children they have to take some sort of legal action. They might take either 'wardship' or 'parental rights proceedings' (see below). If you need help in court proceedings of this kind contact one of the child-care advice groups (see page 181).

A local authority can claim 'parental rights' over a child who is in voluntary care, but only under certain circumstances. The child might have been in voluntary care for three years or more and then the case does not have to go to court. The local authority's social services committee can decide to take on 'parental rights'. They must let parents know by sending them either a copy of the social workers' report or a letter setting out what is in the report. Parents must be told in writing within three days of such a decision being taken. If parents object they should write saying so within one month of getting the letter. If a parent does object the local authority must start legal proceedings in the juvenile court within 14 days.

If the case goes to court parents can be legally represented and should apply for legal aid as quickly as possible. If a resolution is upheld by the court it lasts until the child is 18, but parents can apply to the court for it to be revoked.

Compulsory care

Most children in 'compulsory care' have been taken into care under care orders made in the juvenile court (see page 32). Such orders last until a child is 18 (unless previously discharged). The local authority has 'parental rights' while a child is in compulsory care and can make all important decisions about the child. Parents can contest orders and apply to discharge or revoke orders, and in certain circumstances can apply for access, but they cannot challenge other decisions made by the local authority in the courts. Care proceedings can be brought by the police, the NSPCC (National Society for the Care and Prevention of Cruelty to Children) or by the local authority. Children are entitled to legal representation and may be represented by an independent social worker as well as a solicitor. The court can order that parents should be separately represented as well, in which case they can apply for legal aid. Only children can appeal against the making of a care order. If no guardian has been appointed the parent can appeal on a child's behalf. If a guardian has been appointed the parent cannot appeal at all.

Emergency orders

If it is believed there are grounds for care proceedings children can be removed from their homes in an emergency. In this case there is no court hearing as such although the order for removal is made by a magistrate. This is called a 'place of safety order' and it can last for 28 days. Once the order has expired the local authority must either start legal proceedings or return the child.

The police can remove children for up to eight days without any court order if they think there are grounds for care proceedings.

Access to a child in care

When arrangements are made for a parent to see a child in care they are called 'access arrangements'. Whether you can see your child or how often or for how long depends on the type of care order that has been made. If you are unhappy about access arrangements seek professional advice from one of the child-care advice groups listed on page 181. You can also ask to see a written copy of the local authority's complaints procedure. If your access is stopped altogether the local authority must serve you with a written notice about this. Once you have this notice you can apply to the juvenile court for access to your child. You can be represented by a solicitor and you should apply for legal aid.

Children who are not in care

Wardship

When a child is made ward of court it means that the court has custody and that no important decision about the child's care or well-being can be made without the court's agreement. Unless a wardship is discharged before a child is 18 they remain a ward of court until then. Any interested person (such as a parent or relative) can apply to have a child made ward of court. This is usually done when there is a danger of a child being snatched and taken out of the country, or when relatives or friends are concerned about children and want to look after them, or when children themselves are in dispute with their parents. Parents can be legally represented and should apply for legal aid. When a child is in care or the local authority is starting care proceedings, wardship cannot be used unless the local authority agrees.

Custodianship

Relatives (as well as other people) can apply for custodianship if a child has lived with them for periods of three years or more. If granted it lasts until the child is 18. The person who has custody of the child must consent to the application.

Non-relatives (such as foster parents) can apply for custodianship if children have lived with them for at least one year. The person who has legal custody of the child must consent and this consent must be given on a special form, but it only applies to the application being made and not to the order itself. Custodianship orders can be revoked on application by the parents, the custodian or the local authority. When the court makes a custodianship order it can make an order giving access at the same time.

Custody

A married couple share custody even if they are separated. If the couple have never been married the mother has custody and the father has no rights (though he can apply to the courts for custody). Step-parents have no rights but they can also apply for custody. In disputes between parents over custody, a mother is always entitled to legal representation and should apply for legal aid. Anyone in prison who is involved in a custody application should make sure that their solicitor applies in plenty of time for them to be allowed to attend court. In a case of contested custody the court always decides to do what it thinks is best for the child. Custody and access orders can be changed by the court if one or other of the parents applies for this.

Adoption

Adoption is forever. It cannot be revoked. All rights go from natural parents to adoptive parents. Local authorities can decide that children in care should be adopted if it is not possible for the child to return home in the foreseeable future. In such a case the local authority may find special adoptive parents or may support existing foster parents to help them adopt the child. The parent can either give or withhold their consent, as with adoption. However, a local authority can apply to a court to 'free' a child for adoption. If such an order is made it becomes as if the child has been adopted by the local authority. After that parents are not involved in any further proceedings. Freeing orders can only be revoked in very limited circumstances.

8 Doing 'Life'

A 'life' sentence differs from every other type of sentence and can be the subject of much uncertainty, but three things are certain: because 'life' is indeterminate you will not start your sentence with a release date like other prisoners; everything that happens to you proceeds at a slower pace; and because your sentence will be numbered in years rather than months you are going to need all the resources you can muster to combat the effects of institutionalisation. During a long sentence problems may arise in outside relationships because of the uncertainty of a release date and the fact that it is difficult to keep a partnership going over a period of years in the restricted atmosphere of prison visits. Even where there are solid family or partner relationships, keeping in touch with the outside world is not easy. Ten years is reckoned to be the mark after which the effects of institutionalisation begin to tell. Visits and letters from a voluntary associate (VA) may be especially helpful to anyone in this situation even if they are having other visits. You can read more about who and what VAs are in chapter 7, 'Coping in prison'. Discuss this with the prison probation officer. Many VAs work with and through the probation service, among whom are a voluntary group called Catholic Social Service for Prisoners, who specialise in supportive counselling work with people serving very long sentences. There is also an independent organisation called the New Bridge. You will find all the details on pages 58–60.

Different types of life sentences

'Life' is the only sentence that can be passed for murder, but there are some variations in life sentences.

A mandatory life sentence. The only offence that carries a mandatory life sentence is murder. A judge must impose life on a person who is convicted of murder. It is the only sentence that can be passed.

A discretionary life sentence. Certain offences – such as manslaughter, armed robbery, rape, arson, kidnapping and causing an explosion – may receive a fixed sentence, but the judge has the option of giving life if this is felt to be appropriate. When life is given in these circumstances it is known as a discretionary life sentence. Although you begin your sentence with the same uncertainty about a release date as any other lifer, your tariff date, set by the judge soon after your trial, will be equivalent to the determinate sentence you *might* have received and will not be subject to further consideration by the Home Secretary. The judge's suggestion becomes your tariff date. Your tariff date is not the date at which you will be released, but it does affect your date of release. See below.

A 'recommended minimum'. Sometimes the trial judge in a murder case will make a minimum recommendation of the number of years that should be served when passing sentence. This is not binding and is not a release date. In fact, the 'recommended minimum' means very little at all in real terms since the release of any lifer serving a mandatory life sentence is finally a matter for the Home Secretary. Moreover, its use seems somewhat random since it is by no means always used in the most serious cases. Many people in legal and prison reform circles regard it as little more than an anachronism, a hang-over from the time when capital punishment was abolished and it was felt that the judiciary needed to allay public fears and provide a means of conveying society's abhorrence for certain crimes. However, a 'lifer' who receives a 'recommended minimum' cannot expect to be released before that number of years has passed.

Lifers who can be expected to serve at least 20 years. In 1983 Leon Brittan, then Home Secretary, announced changes in life sentences and detailed certain types of murder for which offenders would be expected to serve at least 20 years. These were:

- murder of a police officer
- murder of a prison officer
- terrorist murder
- sexual or sadistic murder of a child
- murder during the course of a robbery

'Her Majesty's pleasure' (HMP). If you are convicted of murder and were under 18 at the time of the offence your sentence will not be called life but HMP. This is similar to a life sentence but being detained 'during her Majesty's pleasure' means that you may be detained 'in such a place and under such circumstances as the Secretary of State may direct'.

You may also be sentenced to HMP if you are convicted of one of the offences other than murder for which the maximum penalty is life. This means that you will be kept in a secure unit of a local authority home or in a young offender institution during the early part of your sentence rather than in a prison.

Custody for life. If you are convicted of murder (or any of the other offences for which the maximum sentence is life), and are between 17 and 21, you may be sentenced to 'custody for life'. This is the same as a life sentence except that you can be kept in a young offender institution rather than a prison if it is decided that would be a more suitable place.

The first three years

If you are an adult, you will generally first go to a local prison, possibly to the one where you were remanded before trial. You may be there for several months before being allocated to a prison where you will probably spend the first three years of your sentence. The three main lifer centres are at Wakefield, Wormwood Scrubs D Wing and Gartree. After that your moves to other prisons and the time you stay at each one will depend on various factors such as your security category, your general behaviour in prison and also how long you are expected to serve.

Young men between the ages of 17 and 21 will usually go to Aylesbury, Exeter, Swinfen Hall or Castington young offender institution. Women and girls sentenced to life are usually sent to Durham H Wing to start their sentence.

Boys and girls under 17 who are sentenced to HMP may be sent to a young offender institution but are sometimes sent to a local authority community home first. Those who are sentenced to custody for life go to a young offender institution.

In the case of young offenders and juveniles, moves to other places, as with adults, will depend on a number of factors, such as those listed above.

Setting a tariff date

After a murder trial the judge writes to the Home Secretary via the Lord Chief Justice and sets a tariff. The tariff date is not a release date; timing of release depends on other factors as well such as your behaviour in prison and how much of a risk you would be considered to the public if released. What the tariff does is to set the amount of time it is felt you need to serve in order to satisfy the twin objects of retribution and deterrence before other matters are taken into consideration. However, a lifer cannot expect to be released before the tariff date has been reached.

The system for setting tariff dates has changed. Some people who were sentenced to life before the method for setting tariff dates was changed may not have yet been told their tariff date but can expect to hear once the backlog of cases has been cleared.

In discretionary life sentences the judge's suggestion becomes the tariff date. In mandatory life sentences the trial judge's view is only one of the factors the Home Secretary takes into account when setting the tariff. The Home Secretary may decide that the judge has been too lenient and add further time to the tariff. In any event, in the case of any prisoner serving a mandatory life sentence, the decision of the Home Secretary is final.

Your career plan

This plan is a result of discussion between prison staff to map out how it is hoped you will progress towards release. If you start your sentence as Category B your career plan will be started during the first three years of your sentence. If you are Category A discussion about a career plan will not begin until you have been decategorised and gone down to Category B. Your career plan will take into account: the Prison Department's view about the length of time you are likely to serve; your security category; your domestic situation; your needs and any areas of concern; how you are responding to training and the efforts you are making yourself towards education.

Your career plan is not binding and may be altered as time goes on according to your behaviour in prison and other factors both inside and outside the system. You will not be allowed to see it but it will probably be discussed with you in general terms.

The first steps in getting parole

Usually, once your tariff date has been decided, a date will be fixed for your case to be referred to the Local Review Committee as the first step towards parole. This date will usually be timed for three years ahead of the tariff date. This is because the release process is lengthy and if you were to be released at your tariff date some of that time would be spent in preparing you for release. It might be decided that you should go to an open prison or spend some time on the Pre-Release Employment Scheme. So if your tariff is 12 years, your first Local Review date will be at nine years, and if it is more than 20, your first review will be at 17 but you will be told that your tariff is more than 20 years.

Progress reports

Once the date has been set for the first Local Review your case will be looked at regularly within the Prison Department and reports will be compiled at least once every three years by the governor (in association with the assistant governor in charge of your wing), the chaplain, the medical officer, the prison probation officer and anyone else who had had regular contact with you such as a psychologist or case officer. Such factors as your attitude to your offence, your behaviour in prison, contact with family or friends and a probation officer at home (if one has already been allocated), medical records and any particular problems you may have will all form the basis of these reports which will help prison staff to decide when to recommend that you can move a stage further on in your career plan. This may mean a lower security category or a move to more 'open' conditions. These reports eventually form the dossier which is sent to the Local Review Committee who are responsible for the next stage in parole procedure.

Usually there will be internal reviews of your progress around every six months. If you have already been allocated an outside probation officer they will be invited to attend. In some prisons you might also be invited to join the meeting for some of the time. None of these internal reviews have any direct bearing on the timing of your release, but in time the reports which are assembled will go to the Local Review Committee, and eventually to the Parole Board itself.

The Local Review Committee

Every prison has a Local Review Committee (LRC) that conducts the first stage in all parole decisions, not only those of lifers. The committee will consist of the governor of the prison (or a deputy), a member of the board of visitors, a probation officer and at least two other independent people from the local community.

Before the LRC convenes to discuss the case the prisoner also has the opportunity to make a written representation detailing the reasons why he or she considers parole should be granted. If there is a home probation officer they will provide a 'home circumstances' report. The prisoner also has the opportunity of meeting one member of the Local Review Committee (not the prison governor or deputy) for a personal interview. You can refuse to make a written representation or to meet a member of the Local Review Committee, but your case will be considered anyway.

The LRC will have several days to read all the reports and they will read your written representation and hear from the committee member who met you in prison before discussing your case and deciding if they consider you suitable for release.

If they recommend release the case goes to the parole board. If they do not recommend parole the Prison Department may refuse parole without even referring the case to the parole board. The Local Review Committee can also make recommendations about your case, such as a transfer to another prison or more open conditions. They may suggest that if you are released, certain conditions should be written into your licence. However, if the Local Review Committee *do* recommend parole and the case goes forward to the parole board, this does not mean that parole will be granted, nor should it even be seen as a sign that this is likely as it can lead to disappointment. Some lifers and long-termers apply for parole many times.

The parole board

The dossier or file is sent to the Home Office together with any recommendations the committee may have made. If it looks likely that you may be released the views of the trial judge may be sought (if still available) and also the Lord Chief Justice, and then the dossier is sent with this additional information to the parole board.

Members of the parole board perform this duty as a public

service and do not receive any salary or fee. The board is composed of people such as High Court judges, lawyers, psychiatrists or people prominent otherwise in public life, all of whom are invited on to the board by the Home Secretary. They remain on the board for a term of three years.

Each case is considered by the parole board as a panel of five. The panel never meet the prisoner whose case they are considering and make their decision on the basis of the prisoner's dossier and what may have been said at the trial. The board do not have to give reasons for refusing parole but the following factors are known to be considered very important:

- nature of the offence
- criminal and other history
- prison behaviour and response to treatment
- medical considerations
- home circumstances and employment prospects on release
- co-operation with parole supervisor

The parole board also have to try and decide how likely you are to re-offend and whether the resultant publicity might be harmful to the parole system itself if you do. The parole board are extremely aware of publicity and look very closely at notorious cases which might be expected to attract media interest when the prisoner is released. If the parole board do not recommend release but decide that you should remain in prison for the time being they will set the date for your next review. If they do recommend release the case then goes to the Home Secretary.

After the parole board make a decision

If the parole board recommend release the Home Secretary can exercise power of veto. The Home Secretary cannot recommend parole unless the parole board have already recommended it, but no lifer may be granted parole (whatever the findings of the parole board) unless the Home Secretary, who has the final word, is satisfied that the offender is ready to be released. If you have been in prison for over 10 years and release has not been recommended, your case will also be referred to Home Office ministers. However, Home Office ministers have no power to recommend release until the parole board recommend it.

Waiting for the answer is a difficult time and the cause of much tension and anxiety. If a date is not given a prisoner who has already served a very long sentence (over 10 years) and has perhaps waited 18 months or more to hear the result may now show signs of serious stress.

Getting a knockback. When parole is refused it is known popularly as a 'knockback'. The prisoner is given the news in a letter, usually handed over by the prison governor. Perhaps one of the worst things for a lifer who has been refused parole is the feeling that they do not know what to do to improve their chances next time around.

Appeals against a knockback. There is no appeal against the decision not to grant parole. Reasons for refusal are never given. A prisoner will be given no guide as to how to improve the chances of the next application.

A move or an 'early' review. Generally, if the answer has been 'no', the letter from the parole board will give the date of the next hearing. This will most usually be for one year's time. The letter may contain other things, too, such as notification of a move to another prison. If this is to more open conditions the lifer will see this as a hopeful sign. However, it is easy for a lifer to read 'signs' into everything the parole board do or say. When a period of less than one year is fixed for the next parole hearing it is known as an 'early review'. This is also seen as a hopeful sign but it is not a guarantee that parole is in view and should not be taken as such.

Getting a date. Parole is considered to be in sight once a provisional date has been set.

Preparing for release

There may be a possibility of preparing for release by 'working out' at an open prison, getting on to a pre-release employment scheme (see page 117) or getting some home leave.

Short home leave from open prisons. Life sentence prisoners who have a provisional release date (or who have served nine months in open conditions but have not yet been given a provisional release date) may be able to apply for short home leave. They are eligible after four months in open conditions. From then on they can apply every four months and take up to three short home leaves in any 12–month period until eligible for long home leave.

Long home leave. Long home leave is allowed towards the end of a sentence, always subject to the governor's decision. Lifers with a provisional release date or those serving 18 months or more can apply. Long home leave allows five clear days after travelling time. Adults must take long home leave during the last four months of sentence and young people during the last two months of sentence.

Life licence

Once you have been given a provisional date of release you will be assigned a probation officer, unless this has already happened. It is rare, however, for a lifer to be assigned a probation officer until release is in sight.

Before being released you will be read the terms of the licence and asked if you agree to abide by them. The usual conditions of a licence are that the ex-offender shall:

- live only where approved by the probation officer
- inform the probation officer immediately of any change in employment or accommodation
- lead a good and law-abiding life and be industrious

A licence may also contain special conditions. These may include living at a hostel or only living at an address approved by the probation officer, keeping away from certain people or not taking certain types of jobs.

Once you are released you will be on life licence for the rest of your life. For the first part of your licence you will be supervised by a probation officer. You will have to see your probation officer as soon as you are released (an appointment will have been arranged and you must keep it or you put your freedom at risk straight away). After that you will be expected to have very regular contact with the probation service. This means keeping office appointments, allowing your probation officer to visit you at home and not taking any job or moving to a new address without consulting your probation officer. You will also have to ask permission before you travel abroad.

Many lifers find the licence restricting at first, but contact with the probation officer is designed to help you settle back into the outside world. Close supervision during the early part of the licence provides a safety net for any problems that might arise. The probation officer has to send regular reports on your progress to the Home Office and also has to report any problems immediately. If you break your licence by not keeping in touch with the probation officer your licence may be revoked and you will end up back inside.

If everything goes fairly smoothly, then the conditions of your licence may be lifted a few years after you have been released. If this happens you will no longer have to keep in touch with the probation officer but you will still be on life licence. This means that if you get into trouble or your behaviour gives cause for concern your licence may be revoked and you will be sent back to prison.

Recall to prison

The Home Secretary can revoke your licence at short notice and have you recalled to prison, or your licence can be revoked if you are convicted of an offence which carries a prison sentence. The parole board will consider your case and you will be told why you have been recalled. When the Home Secretary recalls a life licensee without prior consultation with the parole board, their confirmation of this decision must be sought as soon as is practicable.

If your licence was revoked by a court the parole board simply looks at your case and decides when it should next be reviewed. If you were recalled for other reasons you will have the chance to make written representations and see a member of the Local Review Committee to explain why you feel you should not have been recalled. Your representations must, by law, be put before the parole board who may order your re-release. If they do not order your release, they will set a date for your case to be reviewed again by the Local Review Committee in the usual way and you will be told when this will happen and given a date for the new review.

9 Partners – the 'prisoners' outside

When a woman's partner commits an offence and receives a prison sentence, it's often said that she becomes a prisoner as well – the 'prisoner' outside. All too often the man's family become the innocent victims of his actions and suffer for something that they have not done. In addition to the problems of keeping a home going and making ends meet, there is the added one of having to make long journeys, month after month, in order to share a brief half hour (trying to keep family life going) under the scrutiny of prison officers. Many loyal women go through this ordeal, sometimes for years on end.

Practical problems and where to go for help

Often a man who goes to prison leaves behind a trail of disaster. There may be arrears of rent or rates, HP instalments to keep up or worries over tenancy. It can be enough of a headache sorting out financial problems at the best of times but it is likely to seem even more of a burden at a time like this. Don't feel you have to do everything on your own and don't be afraid to ask for help. Sometimes just talking things over with someone else can help.

There are many advice agencies that can help with practical problems. There are also support groups run for prisoners' families and a growing number of self-help groups run by women who have either been through, or are going through, a similar experience.

The groups described below will help the partners and families of any prisoner, whatever their colour or nationality. There are also other groups who work specifically for ethnic minority groups. For the full list see pages 180–92.

Prisoners' Wives Service (PWS), the longest established voluntary group of its kind, have been going for 21 years and have a team of women volunteers who visit and befriend women in the Inner London Boroughs. PWS volunteers will visit at home, sometimes just the once to help someone through a crisis, but often on a regular basis throughout the prison sentence. They also give advice, information and general support to the families of people in prison and help them with any of the immediate problems which arise when a family member or close friend is imprisoned. They will continue to give friendship and support while the partner or relation is in prison or for as long as the family welcomes it. They also provide a telephone advice and information service and have two full-time workers available to answer queries on all matters relating to prisons and prison visiting as well as on matters of general welfare rights. They negotiate with the DSS, housing departments or other agencies and will deal with calls from any area. PWS also welcomes callers if they live near enough to drop in. In response to changing needs they are in the process of developing self-help groups where women can support and befriend each other.

Prisoners' Wives and Families was started in 1975 by an ex-prisoner's wife. They offer friendly support and all are welcome to drop in to their friendly North London base during weekdays for a cup of tea and a chat. They will give advice over the telephone to families who are too far away to drop in and suggest you reverse the charge. They can put up homeless women on a short-stay basis in their own hostel and offer a cheap overnight stay to women from out of town who are in London for visits. They also run a holiday scheme for London mothers and children.

Partners of Prisoners and Family Support (POPS) is a self-help group operating in Manchester willing to help anyone from the North of England and North Wales.

The Prisoners' Information Centre operates in the Colchester area. A group called *Help and Advice Line for Offender's Wives (HALOW)* has a national office in Birmingham and other offices in the Southampton and Liverpool areas.

Catholic Social Services for Prisoners are based in London. They visit prisoners in most areas but also offer counselling, practical advice and help to prisoners' families.

Local probation offices will help women form their own self-help groups wherever there seems to be a need. By their nature these groups tend to come and go as people's situations change, so contact your local probation office or CAB for up-to-date details of what is available in your area.

Getting financial help

Social security benefits. If your partner has been claiming benefit for you and for your family it's best to get round to the DSS as quickly as possible to let them know of your changed situation and claim for any extra benefits you might be entitled to.

Income support. Covers living expenses and some housing expenses. You will be entitled to claim this benefit if you are unemployed, or bringing up children on your own, or aged 60 (unless you have more than £6,000 in savings and work more than 24 hours a week). You can also claim if you are staying at home to look after a disabled relative. Go to your local DSS or unemployment benefit office. People in prison cannot claim income support for themselves. No one under 18 can claim unless they have dependants or can show they are estranged from their family or undergoing resettlement.

Housing benefit. You are entitled to this for rent and rates provided you are unemployed or on a low income and you have housing costs or rent and general rates to pay. You cannot claim if you have more than £8,000 in savings. Get the housing benefit form from the DSS or your local authority. The benefit will only cover 80 per cent of your rates. Nothing will be paid for water rates.

Family credit. People who work full time (24 hours a week or over) but who are on low incomes and support at least one child can claim this unless they have more than £6,000 in savings. You will find the form inside the family credit leaflet FC1 obtainable from your local DSS office. Only one member of a couple living together can claim this benefit.

Child benefit. You may be able to claim this but it will affect your entitlement to income support and housing benefit. However, it will be paid on top of family credit.

Guardians' allowance. People who are looking after children without parents can claim this allowance, including someone serving a long prison sentence. If you claim a guardians' allowance it will affect your entitlement to the benefits mentioned above and you cannot get it as well if you are getting one-parent benefit.

Ask at the DSS and get advice from your local CAB or other advice agencies about other benefits available. If you are receiving income support you can get free prescriptions, dental treatment and glasses. Pregnant women and children under five who get income support can have free milk, vitamins and hospital fares. If you get income support your children can also get free school meals. You might be able to get help from the Social Fund in the form of a community care grant. You might also be able to apply for a budgeting loan or a crisis loan which you will have to repay from benefit. Social security law is very complex and you are well advised to contact one of the advice agencies or your local CAB to help you sort out what you are entitled to.

Housing

You cannot be evicted from your home unless a court order is made against you.

Council tenants

Check that your tenancy is secure. If you are married and a council tenancy is in your husband's name get advice quickly from a local CAB or housing advice agency. If the tenancy is in your name only (or in joint names) you should be all right as long as you can pay your rent and rates. Let the housing department know about your change of circumstances.

Private tenants

If you live in private rented accommodation, and the tenancy is in your partner's name but you are not married, the landlord might try to argue that the 'tenant' has abandoned the tenancy. But if you can show that you can pay the rent and rates you may be able to secure the tenancy for yourself. However, you have no *legal* right to take over someone else's tenancy. Seek advice immediately.

Buying your own home

If you (or you and your partner) are buying your own home and you don't earn enough to keep up the mortgate repayments you should check immediately what type of mortgage you have. If it is an endowment mortgage (supported by a life insurance policy in your partner's name) you may be in trouble if the premiums fall into arrears. Contact the building society immediately. They will be glad to offer advice and to try to help you work out some way of keeping your home. It may be possible for the mortgage to be extended or for payments to be frozen for a time. It depends on your individual circumstances. But don't play ostrich. Go and see them and take advice on what's best to do. If you get income support the DSS will only pay 50 per cent of the interest for the first 16 weeks on income support and nothing towards the capital.

If you are homeless

If you have young children or are pregnant go and see the Homeless Persons Unit of your local housing department as soon as possible. If the council agree to re-house you take advice before refusing *any* offer of accommodation. Some councils only allow you to refuse a fixed number of times before they take you off their list. Check whether this applies to your local council.

Go and see your local housing aid centre or contact one of the advice agencies. In an emergency contact Prisoners' Wives and Families who run a short-term hostel for homeless wives in London (see page 90).

Visiting a prisoner

Visiting someone in prison is quite unlike meeting the same person under normal circumstances. You'll be surrounded by people with no chance to be alone. Before you can even set out you must have a VO. Even then you can't just turn up at the prison when you feel like it. Visits are only at certain times and on certain days. You are not allowed to take in food, but you can take cigarettes to smoke during the visit (see page 124).

As soon as you know where your partner has been sent and can arrange it you will want to go and visit him. However, now that he is a convicted prisoner you will need a visiting order. These are *always* called VOs for short. Three adults can visit together on one VO. Adult prisoners are allowed a visit every 28 days. Visits should last at least 30 minutes. In practice most prisons allow two visits each month which may last up to two hours, but prisons vary. You may be allowed extra visits for special reasons. Your partner should talk to the probation officer about this. Sometimes visits can be taken on consecutive days and sometimes a prisoner can be moved to a prison nearer home for visits if his partner or family can't travel. See pages 57–8) for more details about special visits.

The VO (visiting order)

A VO is a printed slip of paper which has been stamped with the name of the prison and the time and days when visits are allowed. Your partner will write your name on it, together with the names of any other adults going with you. Childrens' names do not have to be written on the VO. Your partner will probably send it with a letter. Keep the VO in a safe place. If you lose it or leave it behind on the mantlepiece you may have a wasted journey and get turned away at the prison gates. If this happens read below for information on what to do. If you are on low income or receiving benefits you may be able to get the cost of your visit paid under the assisted visits scheme.

Assisted visits

Close family relatives and partners of prisoners who are either on low income or get income support or family credit from the DSS can claim the cost of a visit every 28 days through the assisted prison visits scheme. So can an adult travelling with the close relative of a prisoner who can't travel alone. However, if the prisoner is serving less than three months you will not qualify for any help from the scheme.

You can sometimes get expenses for a visit you have already made or for emergency visits. You can also claim expenses if you need to stay near the prison because you live too far to make the journey on a regular monthly basis and decide to have a number of visits over a few days. If you are too ill to travel alone (or if a relative of the prisoner is too young to travel alone and needs someone to take them), travelling expenses may be allowed for the person going along to help out.

Ask for form F2022 and the explanatory note F2022A from your local DSS or local probation office. Return the completed

form to the Assisted Prison Visits Unit (see page 187) 10 days
before you wish to visit. Remember to enclose either the VO or
a photocopy. A photocopy is safest. Make sure your partner
does not send a VO too soon after your last visit as it could run
out soon after you send in your application.

The form is easy to fill out and your expenses will be paid
door to door however you travel. If you have to be away from
home for more than five hours you can claim an allowance for
meals. You can also claim for an overnight stay where
necessary. If the prison you are visiting has a hostel for
prisoners' families the unit may send you a voucher or crossed
girocheque made out to the hostel. You may be able to claim
other expenses (such as child-minding) if you can show that
they are necessary. The unit may ask for proof in the form of
receipts. You should get your postage refunded. Payment for
visits is now made direct by the Assisted Prison Visists Unit and
not by local DSS offices. You will either get a Giro or a travel
warrant. If you go in your own car the unit will estimate the
cost of the journey in petrol and pay you that amount by Giro.

Planning and making the journey

When your partner arrives at the prison where he is to start his
sentence, or moves to a new prison, you should get a typed
sheet of directions enclosed with your first letter from your
partner and the VO. Each time he moves to a new prison the
same thing should happen, but things can go wrong and you
may have to set out the first time without having had any
directions from the prison.

You may have a long, tiring journey and still be quite a way
from the prison when you get to the nearest town. Some of the
more remote prisons have special buses to ferry visitors from
the railway or coach station, but not all do. Even when you get
to the visiting room and are sitting together, the visit can be a
let-down if the kids are crying, the baby is fretful or your
stomach is rumbling because you left home early and haven't
had a square meal.

So, if you are visiting a partner or relative regularly, it makes
sense to plan in order to get the best out of your visits. Let the
person you are visiting know in advance when you are coming
and stick to this plan unless there is an emergency. It's no fun
sitting around wondering if someone is going to turn up or not
and your visit will probably be the high spot of your partner's
week. If your partner is not expecting you some of your visiting

time will be wasted while an officer tries to find him. Besides, most prisoners like to prepare for visits and smarten themselves up. It might not matter to you if he can't do this but it will matter to him. It's a question of self-respect.

Going by car

If you are going by car get clear directions for the final part of the journey. Prisons are not noted for having a lot of signs pointing the way and you will not see a signpost until you are almost there. If you have been sent a sheet of directions these may include a rough map showing the way from the prison to the nearest motorway or main route. If you don't get a map ring the probation officer at the prison, your local probation office or local visitors' support/self-help group. They should be able to put you in touch with someone who does know the route. Allow extra time in case you get lost on your first trip to a new prison. Remember to check oil, water and tyre pressure and top up with petrol before you leave. The prison may be off the beaten track. Don't forget, you may be able to claim the cost of the petrol for your journey. (See page 94 for how to claim for assisted visits.) You may be able to share travelling expenses with another visitor if you come across someone who lives near you.

Going by train or coach

Many prisons are difficult to get to by public transport. The local probation service sometimes runs special visitors' coach services. See the Prison Visiting Chart on pages 126–73 for information about transport and other facilities.

   If no special service operates for the prison you are going to, make sure to allow enough time to get from the train or bus station to the prison. It may take longer than you think and it is a waste of valuable time to spend the best part of a day travelling and then miss half your visit by arriving late. If you are going by train check with British Rail about cheap fare schemes. Ask at your nearest station and don't rely on just seeing the information posted somewhere. For some reason BR seem to keep some of their best offers secret. Economy schemes include Inter-City savers for return journeys during off-peak hours and Family Railcards.

Taking children on a prison visit

Children seem to get hungry the minute they step on a train or get into a car, even if they have just had their breakfast! So if you're setting out on a long round trip to a prison with a child make sure you have plenty of picnic food to eat during the journey. Eating in cafés and restaurants is expensive, and there may not be time between trains and buses. It is not just a question of being hungry. Children eat more when they are bored, and hanging around draughty railway or coach stations *is* boring. Make sure there's something you like as well. You'll enjoy the visit more if you're not starving.

The problem of how to occupy children on long journeys is one that all parents have to face at some time or other. Pencils and paper for playing games like noughts and crosses or battleships are a good idea. So are crayons and a drawing pad if you're going by train. Small toys, such as cars or dolls, won't take up too much space. If you're going by car or coach, games like 'I spy' or getting them to count how many red cars they can see in five minutes helps to keep them occupied. Taking a game for children to play with Dad in the visiting room can help to break the ice in those first minutes of a visit. Take a book for younger children and make sure older children take a favourite comic or book. Remember to bring a spare pair of tights and pants for younger children. It's better to be safe than sorry.

Taking a baby

Have a strong, light bag that will hold everything you need for the day and leave your other hand free for the baby and pushchair. Spare nappies (or better still, disposables) are a must. If your baby is bottle-fed, take enough feeds to last the day. Get them ready at home, cool them rapidly and store the bottles in the fridge. When you are ready to leave, pack the bottles into one of those 'cool' bags used for camping and picnics. Germs thrive in milk kept warm for long periods. Don't forget a flask of hot water and some sort of plastic container if you will need to heat the bottle up during the journey. Take some cool, boiled water or diluted rose-hip syrup in case the baby gets thirsty.

If you are breast-feeding remember to take a shawl or scarf to wrap round you both for privacy. Some prisons have visitors' centres where you can change and feed your baby in comfort (see the Prison Visiting Chart, pages 124–73). If your baby is on solids the small jars of babyfood are ideal for a journey. Don't forget to pack a spoon, a bib, some 'wipes' and a plastic bag for odds and ends.

Sometimes the probation service can arrange for a mother with a young baby to have the help of a volunteer (VA) in getting from station or bus station to the prison. Ask your local probation office or local support/self-help group. Visitors travelling across London with small babies should contact Prisoners' Wives Service or Prisoners' Wives and Families who may be able to help.

Staying overnight near a prison

If you have to travel a long way for a visit and can't make the return journey in one day, it's worth knowing that some prisons have local hostels where you can stay at low cost (see the Prison Visiting Chart, pages 126–73). Sometimes visitors can combine a short family holiday with several visits.

Visitors' centres

It's a great help to be able to have a cup of tea and see a friendly face at the end of a long journey. Some prisons have visitors' centres, run by the probation service with the help of local VAs or others. Some centres have a crèche where a mother can leave a baby in safe hands while she has her visit. Visits can sometimes be a strain and a friendly chat over a cup of tea afterwards can be a real boon before facing the long journey home. For details of visitors' centres see the Prison Visiting Chart, pages 126–73.

Arriving at the prison

Aim to get to the prison half an hour before visits start. Getting in to a prison visiting room takes time. Your VO has to be checked and there will be waits between going from gate to waiting room and waiting room to visiting room. It doesn't make sense to spend the best part of a day travelling, only to waste some of your visit by arriving late. Arrangements about going in to the visiting room vary from prison to prison, but the general rule is that in high-security prisons the *prisoner* goes in first and is joined at his table by the visitor, and in open or semi-open prisons the *visitor* goes in first and is joined by the prisoner. According to the way the room is arranged, some tables may give you more privacy than others, and if you are first in the queue you'll stand a better chance of getting a 'better' table. You'll want to make the most of your visiting time as you may have to wait two to four weeks for the next one.

Taking things into a prison

When your partner starts his sentence you should receive a list of articles you can take him. If not, remind him to send a list with his next letter. Each time there is a move to a different prison you should get a new list. It is always up to the individual governor to decide what to allow so prisons vary in this respect. The following are standard at most prisons:

books, magazines, newspapers (magazines and newspapers must usually be sent direct from a newsagent)
a battery-operated radio (only medium and long-wave radios allowed)
watches, battery shavers, calendars and photographs (the inmate must not be on any of the photographs)
a plain gold ring; a St Christophers' medallion
pens or biros

Long-term prisoners can usually have sports equipment and hobby materials. Some prisons allow a battery-operated record player; some allow certain brands of sealed toilet articles (no aerosols). The list will usually say what brands are allowed.

Handing in 'property'

Anything you take for a prisoner is called 'property'. You cannot hand anything direct to your partner but must give the 'property' to an officer who will check individual articles and enter them into a ledger which you will be asked to sign. Everything should be marked with your partner's name and prison number. Different prisons have different routines about handing in 'property'. If you are not sure what to do the first time you go ask an officer or another visitor. In some prisons the rule is that no article can be brought in without first asking permission from the governor, so it is always best to check first when visiting a prison you have not been to before.

Newspapers and magazines will help your partner to keep in touch with the outside world. You can arrange to have daily papers delivered from a local newsagent direct to the prison or pay a subscription and get them sent from the publishers. However, if your partner asks you to arrange subscriptions that you cannot afford, don't be afraid to tell him so. He has probably forgotten how bills mount up. To save money you could take a local weekly newspaper with you when you visit or a supply of those you have had from the previous week. Get him to check first if this is allowed.

Books. Every prison has a library but there may not be much choice. Rules about bringing in or sending books vary from prison to prison. Some prisons only allow new books or books sent direct from a bookshop. In some prisons books must be left in the prison library after they've been read. If your partner starts a new hobby and wants a book on that subject, ask him to check whether second-hand books are allowed and have a look round second-hand bookshops before buying an expensive new book.

Money. You can send money for a convicted prisoner but not take it in with you. Send money by registered post or recorded delivery and keep your receipt. It's not unknown for a prisoner's mail to 'go missing'. Make sure you enclose a note with your name and address on it and mention what you've sent. There are limits on what private cash can be used for and it varies from prison to prison. Check if you are not sure. Generally it can be used to buy newspapers, books and magazines. Some prisons allow private cash to be spent on toiletries. Any surplus cash will be placed in the prisoner's 'property'.

Problems affecting visits

Cancelling a visit

If you find you can't make a visit when you have planned to try to let your partner know you can't come. If it is too late to write, telephone the prison and ask to speak to the probation officer. You'll find the prison telephone number in the Visiting Chart on pages 126–73. Ask the probation officer to have a chat with your partner and explain what has happened. If you have to telephone at a weekend (or some other time when the welfare or probation office is closed), ask if you can speak to an assistant governor or your partner's wing or landing officer. But do remember to write a letter as well explaining why you have not been able to come. Bear in mind that your message may not reach your partner and he may worry even if he does get it. If you have difficulty in contacting the prison one of the groups for prisoners' wives will help out. See page 90.

You arrive to find your partner has been moved

It is not unknown to turn up at a prison expecting to see someone and find they have been moved. If you know in advance that a move is likely it is safest to ring the prison and check first each time just before you go. However, if you arrive to find your partner has been 'ghosted' (moved without warning), try to stay calm. This may not be easy if you have come a long way. Ask the officers at the gate if they know where your partner has been moved to. If not they may be able to arrange for you to see the prison probation officer or someone else who can tell you. Ask someone at the prison to write you a note saying that your partner has been moved. You may need this if you are having assisted visits. If you can't show that this visit didn't take place you may have to wait 28 days for the next one. Keep your VO as you can use it at the next prison.

You can't find out where your partner has been moved to

If your partner has been moved and you don't know where he is, ring or write to the governor and ask him where he has been sent. If the governor can't tell you (though this is not very likely), write to the Prisoners' Location Index (see page 190). The Prisoners' Wives Service or Prisoners' Wives and Families will ring round the prisons and try to find out for you, or try your local group. If you are still having trouble you should write to your MP at the House of Commons explaining that you have taken all the usual steps to find out where your partner is, keeping a copy of your letter. Address it to your MP at the House of Commons. Most MPs have a local 'surgery' to deal with people's problems and you could go to one of these to talk it over in person. The times of such surgeries are usually advertised in the local paper. You can also ask at the local library or CAB, or you can telephone the local party headquarters of your MP and ask for help. You will find the number in your local phone book or Yellow Pages directory. If you write don't forget to mention your partner's full name and prison number.

Your partner has been put on Rule 43

Sometimes a prisoner is segregated from other prisoners by the governor or asks to be separated himself. This is known as 'going on Rule 43'. If this has happened and you are not sure how it will affect your visits, phone the prison and ask to speak to the discipline officer or the probation officer.

Your VO does not arrive in time

Telephone the prison and ask for the probation officer. Give your partner's name and number and explain that your VO has not arrived. The probation officer will be able to check if anything is wrong. If the VO is lost in the post another one can probably be left for you at the gate. If the probation officer is not there, or you can't speak to him or her, ask if you can speak to one of the assistant governors or the wing officer. Only do this if you are due for a visit. If an extra visit is needed for some urgent reason, contact the probation officer or the governor and explain what has happened.

You have lost your VO

If you arrive at the prison to find you have lost your VO or left it at home, explain what has happened to the officer at the gate. The officer will take advice. If you are known there you may still be allowed to have your visit. If so you must post the VO to the prison if you find it at home.

What you can do about problems in the prison

Problems can arise very suddenly in a prison. If you don't get a letter when you expect or just feel something is wrong and can't put your finger on it there could be several explanations. If you are worried (or if something goes wrong at your end and you need to get in touch with your partner in a hurry), ring the prison probation officer who should be able to see your partner and ring you back. He or she might also be able to arrange for you to have a special visit if there is something important you need to talk over.

Some reasons why you may not have heard from your partner

- He may have written to you but the letter may have 'gone missing'. Letters sometimes get lost in the post, or a letter may have been stopped by the prison for some reason or other.

- He may have been moved to another prison at short notice.
- He may be feeling unwell and hasn't written because he doesn't want to worry you or, if he is ill, he may not be able to write. If you are not married this may be a problem since it is up to the governor to decide when and if a prisoner's partner should be told about illness.

How you can find out what is wrong

Ring the prison probation officer. Explain that you haven't heard from your partner at the usual time and you feel something might be wrong. Give his full name and prison number. If the probation officer is out of the office someone else might be able to see him. There might be some simple reason why he hasn't written. If the probation officer senses that something is not quite right but that your partner doesn't want to discuss it with anyone else he might be able to arrange a special visit. This should not affect your normal visiting allowance. However, you can only visit if your partner agrees to see you, so if things have gone wrong between you he *may* refuse.

If your partner has been 'ghosted' or is 'on punishment' or in the punishment block the probation officer should be able to tell you what is going on or whether you haven't had a letter because of some emergency at the prison. You could also ring the prison chaplain and ask if he would see your partner and have a chat. If the probation officer or the prison chaplain ring back to tell you that your partner is ill there are several things you could do to find out more. You might also be able to help in some way.

What you can do to help if your partner is ill

Write to the governor and ask what is happening. If it seems like an emergency you could telephone. Tell the governor that you have been told your partner is ill but would like more information about his condition and what is being done about it. You can also write direct to the prison medical officer to ask what treatment is being carried out. Once you have some idea of what is wrong you could see your family doctor (if he was also your partner's doctor) to talk about your partner's illness. If your doctor knows his medical history he or she might be able to get in touch with the prison medical officer and find out what treatment is being given. The doctor might even be able to help by passing on information about your partner's previous medical history.

If there is no family doctor who can help, talk to one of the advice agencies (see pages 186–92). Remember that things can go wrong sometimes and a second opinion might be needed. Someone with more experience of the system may be able to suggest something that can be done.

What to do if you suspect drug treatment

If your partner seems very depressed or looks different and you suspect he may be having a drug that doesn't agree with him, talk to someone in one of the advice agencies on pages 186–92.

What to do if you are still worried

Get in touch with your MP. Write to the MP at the House of Commons (see page 180), and don't forget to keep a copy of your letter. Give your partner's full name and prison number and as much information as you can. Follow the steps for getting in touch with your MP listed on page 101.

Keeping in touch

Often it is difficult to feel relaxed with someone when you only see them for a short time every month, however well you knew each other before the sentence started. You and your partner are no longer sharing the same daily life. His day is a bit of a mystery to you and he can only guess how things are for you. The worst of visits is that you just start to feel relaxed with one another when they call 'time' and you're heading for the train again.

If you can write regular letters to each other it will be easier to keep in touch with one another's daily lives. Not everyone finds letter writing easy. It can help to try to think of a letter as a way of talking on paper. Put down whatever comes into your head such as the funny things the kids said on the way to school. The best letters are not those with perfect grammar and spelling but the ones which make the person who wrote the letter come alive as if they are in the room while it is being read. This kind of chatty letter will help to keep your partner in touch with what is going on at home.

Try to be as honest with each other as you can from the beginning. You are both in an unreal situation but you don't have to make it even more unreal by protecting your partner too much. Don't make your letters one long moan (that would only make him feel guilty), but don't protect him from your problems and shut him out of your life. If he can help, even by listening, he'll feel he is still part of the family.

Letters you send to your partner are not read in open prisons, and in category C prisons only about 5 per cent of letters are read by the censor. Otherwise, remember your partner will be aware of the censor and keep private family matters for visits.

Remember that your partner has pressures, too, and won't want to talk much about prison life. However, there might be worries you could share such as what he is going to do when he comes out. If he is worrying about finding a job you could tell him about the two groups that help ex-offenders get work after release. They will sometimes send someone to talk about employment prospects before a prisoner is released (see pages 119–120).

It is hard to say why some couples stay together even through a long sentence and others don't. There is no doubt that when a man goes to prison for a long time it puts a strain on a relationship. Anyone who is locked up is bound to lose contact with reality occasionally and prisoners often do retreat into fantasy. If this happens, be understanding but try to keep your feet on the ground at the same time.

Have visits alone sometimes. Don't feel you have to take the children with you every time you go. Take advantage of childminding offers from family or friends. If you have no one you can leave them with, one of the partners' support or self-help groups may be able to help.

If one child is having difficulties at home and maybe getting into trouble at school you might think about taking that child alone on a visit so they can feel special. As well as being good for the child it will help your partner to feel he is playing his part, too.

If things go wrong, or if you reach a point where you feel that you can't carry on any longer, don't leave it until the day your partner comes out to tell him. If you are feeling under strain do get in touch with one of the support groups. It helps to talk things over, especially with someone who has been in the same situation (see pages 89–91).

When your partner is coming up for parole a probation officer will be asked to prepare a special report for the parole board called a 'home circumstances report'. The probation officer will want to come and see you at home for a chat. The chance of a previous job being taken up again or a new one in the offing might help his chances of parole. Discuss this with the probation officer.

If your partner is refused parole, or 'gets a knockback', don't feel it is your fault. If he should lash out and blame you, remember that people who cannot give vent to feelings of frustration (and nothing is more frustrating than being locked up) are inclined to lash out at their nearest and dearest.

Getting used to each other again

When the great day comes and your partner is released it is easy to see it as an end to all your troubles. Remember that you will both have to adjust to one another again and as nothing stands still in life you will both almost certainly have changed.

When your partner went away you may have wondered at first how you were going to manage, but if you have got used to making all the decisions it isn't going to be easy to let him take over again. You may say 'Why should I?', but if you seem not to need him he may feel there is no place for him now. Try to talk things over and see each other's point of view. That way you'll be working together and not pulling in opposite directions.

If he doesn't come out to a job remember that rejections are likely at a time of high unemployment and be as supportive as you can. If he can't find a job it doesn't mean he is not looking for work. Trying to find work is no joke for anybody who is unemployed, but if he has got used to having everything done for him it will be even harder for him than the next man.

While your partner was in prison he will have talked a lot about how much he wanted to be back home with you, but once the novelty wears off he may revert to old habits and start to spend time with his mates. If this happens try to avoid resentment but don't be a doormat. You will probably have taken up new interests and made new friends while he was inside. Don't drop them, and give your relationship time to adapt to all the changes that have taken place.

Part III
Coming Out

10 Release

The day of release, anticipated and longed for, can be a time of great anxiety and stress when it finally arrives. The outside world may seem hostile and unpredictable at first after a life of routine within four walls. In many ways one institution is much like another and anyone who has stayed in hospital for a time will remember how it feels to emerge from a quiet ward into crowded noisy streets. A relatively short journey in a car can induce nausea and panic in someone who has become unused to going faster than their own two feet can carry them, and even prisoners who have served only a short sentence can find the impact of the outside world alarming after the slower pace of prison life.

Adjustment is especially difficult for those who have no established home to go to, and therefore preparation for release is vital if you are homeless. See the prison probation officer well before the release date and press for help in finding somewhere to live. This will give you a realistic chance of keeping your cool and fulfilling any promises you may have made to yourself about staying 'out' this time. Unfortunately those most in need of help are also least likely to ask for it. It's worth bearing in mind that the probation service is overworked, and since most probation officers are hard-pressed and not mind-readers, they won't know that you need help unless you tell them.

Once the probation officer knows your situation he or she will be able to contact the local office in the area where you intend to live and make arrangements for you to get help in finding somewhere to live. Offenders who come from an area outside the 12 Inner London boroughs (but who wish to come to London on release) will, in general, be dealt with by the probation After-Care and Resettlement Group (Inner London

Probation Service) (see page 188). Those sentenced within Inner London, who are homeless and rootless, will be dealt with by the team who cover the local magistrates' court for the area within which they were sentenced.

If there is a chance of a room in a hostel or a place in some project suited to your particular needs, you may be able to get some home leave to pay them a visit and find out if your face 'fits'.

An offender without home or family may find the friendship of a VA a particular support at this time. Where there is no statutory probation order the VA may, at the very least, be useful for jogging the memory of the appropriate person and making sure that an ex-offender who is diffident about asking gets help when it is needed.

The release date

Working out release dates can be complicated. Periods spent on bail and in custody before sentence was passed will be regarded as counting towards time served. Normally, part of your sentence will be 'remitted' (or pardoned) for good behaviour. Remission is not to be confused with parole and it is automatic for all sentences except 'life', including those served in young offender institutions.

You should be told of your earliest date of release (EDR) within 24 hours of being sentenced and, if all goes well, that should be the date when you are finally released. However, you can 'lose' remission as a punishment. The EDR is half your sentence if you are doing 12 months or less (unless that leaves less than five days), and two-thirds of your sentence if you are doing more than 12 months.

Getting parole

If you are serving more than 12 months and have at least seven months to go after sentence (taking remission into account), you will also be eligible for parole. When you are told your EDR and last date of release (LDR) you will also be told the date at which you will become eligible for parole (PED). This is the earliest date you could possibly be released on parole. It will either be six months after the date of your sentence, or when a third of the sentence (counting time on remand) has been served – whichever is the longer. But – unlike remission – parole is not automatic, and being eligible for parole does not mean it will be granted. There is a process to be gone through and the complexity and length of the process depends on the length of sentence being served. Obviously, the longer the sentence the greater the importance of parole to the individual prisoner.

Prisoners who are eligible for parole fall into two types:

- those serving fixed sentences of less than two years, who are dealt with under section 33
- those serving fixed sentences of two years or more who fall under section 60

All parole involves reports being made by probation and prison staff and collected into a dossier or file which will then be considered by a committee of people known as 'the Local Review Committee'. However, in the case of prisoners serving longer sentences, that is only the beginning of the parole process.

The Local Review Committee

The Committee is composed of the prison governor (or deputy), a local probation officer, a member of the Board of Visitors and two local people who have no other connection with the prison. Reports are prepared over a period by prison and probation staff. These reports form part of the prisoner's file or dossier and will include details of how the offender has behaved in prison and their home circumstances. The prisoner can also write a short report stating why they want parole and what they plan to do when they get out. One committee member (not the prison governor) meets the prisoner in person in case there is anything he wants to add to what he has written himself.

After the committee have had time to read and consider all the papers they meet together to discuss the case and hear from the member who has met the prisoner. They then decide whether that person is suitable to be released early.

All section 33 cases are decided by the Local Review Committee and some longer-term cases may be decided by them, but on the whole these will go on to the parole board for further consideration.

The parole answer

If you come under Section 33 parole (or your case is being decided by the Local Review Committee anyway), you will normally be told the result of your parole hearing about three or four weeks before your parole eligibility date (PED). However, this does not happen in all cases and sometimes this date is passed before the result arrives. Sometimes there may be an indication of a move to another prison and more open conditions instead of just a straight 'yes' or 'no'. Another possibility is to be given a 'late date' or an 'early review'.

A late date is basically a 'yes', but it will be dated some time after your PED and before your EDR. You might be serving 18 months and hoping for six months' parole before the sixth–month (PED) and the twelfth–month (EDR) points of your sentence. If the Local Review Committee decide that you should only have three months' parole, you would be told at about five months that you would be released on parole when you have done nine months of your sentence.

An early review means that if you are hoping for section 60 parole your case will be reviewed again by the parole board before the usual 12–month period between reviews is up. If you are refused section 60 parole you can apply for an early review, but this may be refused if there are no valid grounds such as a major change in your situation.

Getting a 'knockback'. A parole refusal is known popularly as a 'knockback'. Usually you will hear via a letter handed over by the prison governor. If you are refused parole you can apply again between 10 and 12 months after the date of the last LRC meeting as long as there is at least 16 months left between the last LRC meeting and your EDR. There is no appeal against a 'knockback' and reasons are never given.

The parole licence

Parole is only given subject to certain conditions known as the 'parole licence'. All ex-offenders released on parole are expected to:

- report to their probation officer as and when required. (The first appointment is very important as the probation officer has to notify the Home Office that you have been seen and let them know your address.)
- live only at a place approved of by the probation officer and tell their probation officer immediately of any change of address or employment

- lead a law-abiding and industrious life

Sometimes special conditions are attached to a parole licence.

An ex-offender on parole who does not keep to the terms of the licence runs the risk of being recalled to prison even without committing another offence. The probation officer would have to apply to the Home Office and the decision for recall must be made or confirmed by the parole board. However, recalls can take place quickly in an emergency.

An essential condition of parole is a good relationship with the probation officer who will be in charge of overseeing the parole licence.

The probation service

The probation and after-care service began as a voluntary agency run by missionaries in the 19th century police courts, and later became part of the criminal justice system operated by British courts.

Probation officers became responsible for supervising offenders released on parole by the Home Office for the first time in 1967. Today there are thousands of probation officers in England and Wales under the direct responsibility of the Home Secretary. There are probation officers who work with the courts and supervise offenders after release as well as others who now work in every prison in the country.

The probation service works in two ways for ex-offenders: there is a statutory duty to provide after-care for ex-offenders who have either been released on parole or placed on probation by the courts and sometimes probation will be specified by the court as an alternative to going to prison. Under any of these circumstances the ex-offender has a statutory duty to keep contact and observe the terms of the licence or probation order. In addition, there is a statutory duty on the part of the service to provide after-care for any ex-offender who requests it on a voluntary basis for a period of up to one year after release. In this case the relationship is statutory only as far as the probation officer is concerned, and the ex-offender is not obliged to keep contact. Anything that will help the ex-offender re-settle into the community is termed 'after-care'. This might mean talking over problems or helping to find a job or somewhere to live.

Parole for long-termers

Certain changes in parole policy which affected offenders serving longer terms were introduced in 1983 by Home Secretary Leon Brittan when he announced that offenders serving prison sentences of five years and over for offences involving drug trafficking, sex, arson or violence would not normally be considered for release until the end of their sentence.

Parole for those serving a long sentence is similar to that for lifers. For further details about the parole process for long-termers see pages 83–6.

A young offender institution licence

Every offender who is released from a young offender institution (YOI) is on licence when they get out and must have regular contact with a probation officer or social worker, usually between the EDR and the LDR. This licence lasts for three months. The longest a YOI licence can run is 12 months. If you come out of a young offender institution you will be on licence for three months even if this goes past your LDR.

If you get released from a young offender institution on parole, then your YOI licence follows your parole, but the parole time counts towards the 12 months you will be on licence. If your probation officer or social worker thinks you have broken the conditions of your YOI licence then they have to take you to the magistrates' court to prove it. You can then be fined up to £200 or sentenced to up to 30 days in custody.

Preparing for release

One way of preparing for release is to be granted a spell of home leave. You must make an application for home leave and it is up to the governor to decide whether you should be granted leave or not. Prisoners serving fixed sentences of 12 months and over and certain life sentence prisoners become eligible for home leave towards the end of their sentences. However, it is important to understand that leave from prison is a privilege and not a right.

Short home leave

Short home leave is available to adults serving sentences of three years or more at a closed prison. It is intended to be used for re-establishing home contacts. Short home leave can only be taken when you are into the last nine months leading up to your EDR. However, once you have passed this point you can apply any time up until the time when you become eligible for long home leave. Short home leave is usually taken over a weekend and allows two clear days in addition to travelling time.

Men from Category C prisons or women from Bullwood Hall, Cookham Wood, Styal or New Hall who are serving a fixed sentence of two years or more can apply for short home leave once they reach the date when they become eligible for parole. After that they can apply every six months until they become eligible for long home leave. After that they can take up to two home leaves in every 12-month period. This type of home leave does not normally apply to lifers. However, if you are a 'lifer' and have a provisional release date you can apply for short home leave, but you will not be able to take this until you are into nine months before your EDR and until you qualify for long home leave.

Fixed sentence prisoners serving a sentence of 18 months or more at an open prison can apply to take short home leave at any time after they become eligible for parole.

Young offenders are eligible for short home leave in roughly the same way as adults. Those in 'open' young offender institutions can apply for up to three leaves a year; those who are in 'closed' young offender institutions are eligible in the same way as adults in Category C. The exceptions to this are young offenders at Swinfen Hall, Castingdon, Aylesbury, Grendon and other prisons and remand centres. If you come into this last group you must be serving three years or more to become eligible.

Long home leave

Long home leave can be taken towards the end of a sentence, always subject to the governor's decision. Lifers with a provisional release date or those serving 18 months or more can apply. You can have five clear days after travelling time. Adults must take long home leave during the last four months of sentence and young offenders during the last two months of sentence.

If you are a young offender serving a fixed sentence of 12 months or more you can apply for long home leave which, if it is granted, can be taken in the eight weeks before your EDR. You must have served at least three months to be considered for long home leave.

Pre-parole leave

If you are serving a fixed sentence of 18 months or more and
have been granted parole you can apply for pre-parole leave.
You will be allowed two clear days plus travelling time. To
become eligible you must be within four months of your parole
release date or there must be less than three weeks left to serve.
If you are eligible for pre-parole leave you will not be eligible
for short or terminal home leave.

The conditions for pre-parole leave for young offenders are
the same as for adult offenders.

Temporary release

Temporary release can be granted by the governor. Generally
this will either be granted on compasionate grounds to enable
you to attend the funeral of a close relative or visit someone
who is seriously ill, or for some matter connected with preparation
for release that cannot be dealt with from prison.

Young prisoners in young offender institutions may be
allowed various kinds of temporary release to allow them to
attend a course or college of some kind. There can be a wide
variety of options and young offender institutions may offer
different activities such as outward bound courses or participation
in community service projects.

Conditions and financial help for home leave

A prisoner who wants to take home leave has to provide a
suitable address which will be checked by a probation officer.

If you are granted home leave you will be given a travel
warrant and any necessary money for extra travel from your
home-base address such as going to see about a job. You
should also get an allowance for food for the journey or be
provided with a packed meal. If the home leave is to be spent
in a hostel or lodgings the prison will pay for the cost of
accommodation and meals. If a prisoner is going to stay with a
partner, family or friends, they may be able to apply for a
community care grant but only if they are already receiving
income support. If they are not receiving income support the
Prison Department might allow a small amount of cash to help
out with the cost of the stay. If you think that you will need this
apply as soon as possible to the governor or prison probation
officer.

Section 53 prisoners

Section 53 (2) of the Children and Young Persons Act 1933
allows for Crown Courts to impose sentences of longer than 12
months on juveniles (young people below the age of 17). These
sentences are different from normal fixed sentences in a number
of ways. If you are a section 53 prisoner:

- you can be released on licence at any time during your sentence
- you have an LDR but no EDR
- your release date depends on how the Parole Board sees
  your progress
- you remain on licence after release until the date of the end
  of your sentence

There is no set date for the parole board to review your case for
the first time. It will usually take place about three months
before you reach the one-third mark in your sentence. If your
sentence is four years or longer the parole board may decide to
ask for a progress report before that date. When your first
review takes place the parole board will set the time for your
next review if they decide not to grant you release.

If you are not serving a life sentence you can apply for long
or short home leave in the same way as anyone in a young
offender institution serving a sentence of the same length. You
will only be allowed to take long home leave if you have been
given a date for release on licence or if you are coming up to
the end of your sentence. If you are to be released on licence in
the usual way you will be able to apply for two days temporary
release in order to prepare for it.

Pre-release employment

One way of preparing for release, especially if you have been
serving a long sentence, is to be allowed to go out of prison to
work during the day, in the months leading up to your release
date. These pre-release employment schemes generally operate
in open prisons and there is also a hostel at Pentonville prison
and Wormwood Scrubs in London where offenders can live in
and work out during the day. It is a condition of being on the
hostel scheme that you must have a job. If you want to go on
this scheme it's best to apply as early as possible.

Getting out

Most prisoners should receive a discharge grant and a travel warrant when they are released. The amount of the discharge grant you can expect to get depends on your age and on whether you will be returning to a home address or will be homeless. Prisoners under 16 will not get a discharge grant. There is no grant for anyone serving less than 14 days. The other categories who can not expect a discharge grant are remand prisoners, fine defaulters, civil prisoners and those awaiting deportation or travelling to an address outside the UK. There are several bands of payment. For further information, consult the Prison Reform Trust's 'Prisoners' Information Pack' or the Women Prisoners' Resource Centre's 'Reception Pack' (see page 193).

You will normally be released in the early hours and certainly before 8 a.m. People talk about getting 'gate fever' as the time of release draws near. Others fear 'gate arrest', particularly if they have refused police interviews during their sentence. If this is going to happen the governor is supposed to let the inmate know in advance so that any family or friends planning to meet them at the gate on the day of release can be told and saved from turning up for an early morning meeting for nothing.

Getting financial help

As an ex-prisoner you are in one of the priority groups for community care grants. You might get a grant for clothing if, for instance, you have no coat to keep you warm. If you are moving into a new home you might get help for essential furniture, household items or bedding.

Signing on

You should go to the DSS as quickly as possible (it's best to go on the day you are released) so that you can get your benefits sorted out with as little delay as possible. Many offenders find it difficult to queue up patiently and answer a lot of questions when they have just been released from prison, but it's best to keep your cool and get it over and done with speedily so that you don't lose out on any benefits you are entitled to. Income support is paid fortnightly and in arrears so you will not receive this money for the first two weeks. Your discharge grant does not count as payment for the first week but you will still have to manage until you get your delayed income support. If you run out of money go to the DSS and ask for a crisis loan. You will have to pay this back and the payments will be taken out of your giro automatically every fortnight. If this does not go smoothly and you are still having problems and don't have enough money to feed yourself or pay for a bed, go to your local probation office (see pages 109–10 if you are not sure which office you should go to).

Getting back into the job market

There are two voluntary organisations which were set up for the purpose of helping ex-offenders find jobs and between them they have helped many hundreds of prisoners get back into the job market. Today, in a period of high unemployment, this kind of help is more necessary than ever before. Any ex-offender who is serious about wanting to find a job and make a fresh start is well advised to approach these organisations which are independent of the statutory agencies.

Apex Trust

Originally set up by an ex-offender, Apex Trust have been going nearly 25 years. Their long experience in helping ex-offenders back into employment makes their service the highly professional operation that it is today. They have six training centres across the country as well as a head office in London.

They operate in a number of ways. At a basic level they will help in filling in application forms and in preparing for interviews, but they also offer occupational training and assist people who want to get into self-employment. They run two-day pre-employment courses in prison during the last two months of sentence. They also work together with New Bridge.

New Bridge employment service

The New Bridge employment service started in 1971. They also befriend prisoners and visit prisons (see pages 58–9 to find out more about this aspect of their work).

Ex-offenders are asked to make an appointment first and then come in for an interview. This is important as they need to know if a prospective client is committed enough to finding a job to be able to make the first step by keeping the appointment.

A client who cannot keep this appointment is likely to find it difficult to get themselves along to an interview with a prospective employer, when pressure will be that much greater. Like Apex Trust, New Bridge will contact employers and set up interviews. They will also prepare CVs for those with the right kind of experience. A small charity with limited resources, they can only offer their full service to people who live in the Greater London area or within reasonable commuting distance, but they will advise ex-offenders from any area. They also work with Apex Trust.

NACRO

NACRO run a number of Community Programme schemes which give employment and training to thousands of ex-offenders (as well as other long-term unemployed people) for periods of up to 12 months. They also run a Youth Training scheme with projects providing a two-year programme of training and planned work experience. Talk to your probation officer or local probation office about this or contact NACRO direct.

For how to contact these organisations see pages 186–9.

Making a fresh start

In prison you will have got out of the habit of dealing with day-to-day problems: decisions were made for you whether you liked it or not and there were no rent or food bills to worry about. Add to this that you have probably forgotten what a long time it takes to get from one place to another and that there will almost certainly be a lot of waiting about leading to a fair amount of frustration. What you are having to cope with is the after-effects of institutionalisation and it will get better. If you made yourself promises while you were away about making a go of things this time and not going back inside, recognise that you will probably need some support and don't be afraid to ask for help. A look at the list of support organisations for ex-offenders and their partners on pages 186–92 will show you that there is plenty of help available.

The good news is that you can truly make a fresh start as far as some sentences are concerned. However, the rules which govern which sentences become 'spent' and when are complicated. You will find all the information on this subject on pages 175–9.

The problem about anything in life that gets built up in one's mind by having to wait for it – and release from prison certainly comes into that category – is that there can be a feeling of let-down when the waiting is over. Coming out of prison is not the only time when people focus on one event in this kind of way: it can happen when you are waiting for an operation or having a baby. Some people feel the same way about moving or starting a new job: everything was supposed to be perfect suddenly and it isn't. All the other problems have been put on hold and it can be a nasty shock when they surface again with a rush. The best way to cope with this period of adjustment is not to try to do everything all at once and deal with it the same way as you did with your sentence, one day at a time.

Part IV
Prison Visiting Chart

All prisons in England and Wales are listed together with address, telephone number, category, times and days when visits can be made and any available extra details about visits, such as whether the visiting time is designated for domestic or professional (legal) purposes.

Where there are special transport facilities (coach or minibus services organised by the probation service), details and contact phone numbers are given as available. Usually visitors can be picked up at central points and taken to the prison and back. Although the list is as complete as possible at the time of going to press, services can be cancelled or new ones set up and it is always best to check before setting out. Contact the prison and ask for the probation department or the discipline officer. You could also check with your local probation office or one of the prisoners' wives groups.

You may not take any item of food into the visiting room to offer to a prisoner, but most prisons have a canteen to sell tea or coffee in the visits room, and usually there will be biscuits or light snacks which you can purchase for yourself and the prisoner you are visiting. You can take cigarettes to smoke during the visit (except at young offender institutions where neither 'trainees' nor visitors are allowed to smoke), and you may offer these to the prisoner you are visiting, but you may not hand over cigarettes to take back into the prison. It is a serious offence and carries a term of imprisonment or a fine or both. This rule also applies to any 'unauthorised' article which means in fact that you can hand over nothing at all. You can take certain items of 'property' in for a prisoner and, in certain prisons and certain circumstances, you can take toilet articles. For further details about visiting, including what you can take in for a prisoner, see pages 99–100. For any problems connected with visits such as losing a VO (visiting order), or other problems that can arise when visiting a prison, see pages 100–102.

Facilities for children vary: some prisons provide a proper crèche, others have a play area, and there may be toys in or near the visiting room, but some prisons have no facilities at all for children. Disabled visitors may find access difficult at many prisons although usually officers will, if asked, help to lift wheelchairs upstairs. Check first with the probation officer at the prison in case of difficulty.

Visitors' centres, usually sited outside the prison, are places to go to unwind after a visit. Most have workers or volunteers who offer support and advice. Some centres may be able to provide child-minding during the visit. At some prisons there are probation hostels nearby where families can stay overnight. Check details with the prison probation officer and book as early as possible, especially during busy holiday periods.

The Prison Visiting Chart which follows on pages 126–73 is the copyright of the Prison Reform Trust and reproduced by kind permission of the director, Stephen Shaw.

Abbreviations

P   HM Prison
RC   HM Remand Centre
YOI   HM Young Offender Institution

Type of Prison	Category	Visiting Times	Public Transport	Special Transport
P **ACKLINGTON** Morpeth Northumberland NE65 9XF 0670-760411	C	1.30–4.30 pm daily. No admission after 3.30 pm	Train to Newcastle upon Tyne. Metro to Haymarket. X18 bus takes an hour	From West Yorks, Cleveland, Manchester, Merseyside, S. Yorks via probation service
P **ALBANY** Newport Isle of Wight PO30 5RS 0983-524055	B Dispersal	2–4 pm daily	Train to Portsmouth then ferry to Ryde or train to Southampton and ferry to Cowes then bus	Coach from London every Sunday. Bookings tel. 01–407 7013
P **ALDINGTON** Ashford, Kent TN25 7BQ 023372-436/7	C&D	2–4 pm Wed, Sat, Sun	Train to Ashford Bus 525, 526 to Aldington from Vicarage Lane, Taxi £6 each way from train station. See also notes for extra bus service	None
RC ASHFORD Woodthorpe Rd Ashford, Middx TW15 3JZ 0784-241041		Mon–Sat, 1.30–3.30 pm		
P **ASHWELL** Oakham Leicestershire LE15 7LF 0572-56075		Daily 30 mins between 1.00-3.30 pm. Longer visits on Sat, Sun & 2nd & 4th Wed of the month	Train to Oakham (Birmingham/ Peterborough line) then train or walk. Barton's bus no.2 from Nottingham	From Birmingham, Coventry, Leicester, Chesterfield and Northampton – contact probation
P **ASKHAM GRANGE** Askham, Richard York, N. Yorks YO2 3PT 0904-704236	Women's Open	Sat and Sun 1.45–3.15 pm. Visits during week only, 30 mins and must be booked	Train to York then infrequent 87 bus or taxi £5 each way. Tadcaster bus from Leeds	None

Visitors' Centre	Canteen	Kids' Play Area	Overnight Stay	Notes
No	Mon Wed, Sat Sun	Yes	Contact prison probation	Half mile walk from bus stop. No shelter for early arrivals
No	Daily	Yes	Short and long stay. Contact prison probation	Disabled access very difficult as visiting room is upstairs and there are narrow doorways
No	Yes	No	None	Bus from Vicarage Lane (opposite old bus station) 12.20 pm weekdays. 1 pm Sat – returning from Aldrington 4.21 pm
Yes				
No	Available on long visit days	Yes		
No	At weekends	At weekends	None but plenty of B&Bs in York	Wheelchair ramp available

Type of Prison	Category	Visiting Times	Public Transport	Special Transport
YOI Bierton Rd **AYLESBURY** Bucks HP20 1EH 0296-24435	Young Offenders (long term)	1.30–3.30 pm Wed, Sat, Sun	Train to Aylesbury Taxi or foot from town centre	Coach from London on Sundays when demand is sufficient. Tel. 01–837 4390
P St Loyes St **BEDFORD** MK40 1HG 0234-58671	B Local	1.30–3.30 pm daily. Remand prisoners no Sun visits but Sat visits also 9.30–10.30 am	Train/bus to Bedford	None
P Winson Green Rd **BIRMINGHAM** B18 4AS 021-554 3838	Local	Remand prisoners: Mon to Sat 1.00-2.30 pm. Convicted prisoners: Tues, Thurs, Fri and Sun 1.00– 2.30 pm	New St Station Buses 82, 87 & 88 to Summerfield Park, Dudley Rd. (then 5 mins walk) or 76 from Bull St City Centre	None
P **BLANTYRE HOUSE** Goudhurst Cranbrook Kent TN17 2NA 0580-211367	C	Tues, Wed, Thurs & weekends 2–4 pm	Train to Marsden (4-mile journey)	Minibus meets last train before 2 pm most days. Phone prison for specific lifts
P **BLUNDESTON** Lowestoft Suffolk NR32 5BG 0502-730591	B	1.45–3.45 pm daily, Sundays crowded	Lowestoft Station Prison van collects visitors on Wed, Sat and Sun £1. Otherwise taxi	Coach from London on Sundays calls at Chelmsford and Colchester. Book on 01–237 2707
P BRISTOL Cambridge Rd Horfield Bristol BS7 8PS 0272-426661	B	Mon to Sat 1.30–3.30 pm. Long-term wing 1.30–3.30 pm daily	Bus 8 or 9 from Temple Meads to Debenhams. Then 75, 77 or 78 from Bristol Fashion shop to Bishop Road	None

Visitors' Centre	Canteen	Kids' Play Area	Overnight Stay	Notes
12.30–1.30 pm on winter Sundays at Tindal hospital chapel	Yes	No	B&B available locally	Disabled access difficult but arrangements can be made with advance notice
	Yes for convicted. No for remand			No wheelchair ramps but access quite easy. Clothing exchanges for unconvicted prisoners not allowed all day Sat
Yes	Yes for convicted. No for remand	Yes, in visitors' centre	None	All visitors must book in at vistors centre opp. prison – from 11.30–2.30 pm. Wheelchair access. Refreshments, creche and info centre
No	Yes	Yes	Could arrange local B&B	No steps to visitors' centre. Therefore disabled access no problem
No	Yes	Yes – with video cartoons	Contact prison probation for local guest houses	No wheelchair ramps but easy access to visits room
No	Yes	Yes – weekdays only	Book through Family Centre Warden, phone 0272-425994	No provision for wheelchairs

Type of Prison	Category	Visiting Times	Public Transport	Special Transport
P Jebb Aven **BRIXTON** London SW2 5XF 01–674 9811	B Remand	Mon to Fri 9.15–11.15 am, 1–3.45 pm, Sat 9.15–11.15 am, 1–3 pm. No Sunday visits	Underground to Brixton, then bus 50, 95, 109, 133, 159 southwards to Jebb Ave	None
RC BROCKHILL Redditch Worcestershire B97 6RD 0527-550314	B	Mon to Fri, 1.30–3.30 pm; Sat, 1.00–3.00 pm. No Sunday visits	Birmingham Bus Station to Redditch 147 bus. Redditch to Hewell Park 318 bus	From Wolverhampton and Birmingham tel. 0902–710621 to book; Coventry, tel. 0203–29240
YOI BUCKLEY HALL Buckley Rd Rochdale OL12 9DP 0706-58094	Senior DC	Mon, Wed, Thurs, Sat and Sun 1.30–3.30 pm	Rochdale Bus station, buses no. 454, 455, 457 to Red Lane	None
P BULLINGTON Patrick Haugh Rd Arncott Bicester Oxon OX6 0PZ				Due to open January 1991
YOI & P BULLWOOD HALL High Rd Hockley Essex SS5 4TE 0702-202515	Closed Female	9.30–11.00 am, 1.30–3.00 pm daily	BR Eastern Region Liverpool St – Rayleigh. Then bus 7 or 8 to Bullwood Lane or taxi from 'BESTAX' office immediately outside front entrance to station	None

Visitors' Centre	Canteen	Kids' Play Area	Overnight Stay	Notes
Yes	Yes	No	None	No facilities for disabled access. Access is possibe but very difficult. Only three adults and two children under 16 (older children count as adults). Only one visit per day. Saturdays are very crowded. No prams or pushchairs in prison or visitors' centre
Yes	Yes	Yes	None	No disabled access Maximum three visitors
No	Yes – at weekends	No	None	No disabled access Maximum three visitors. No smoking
No	Yes at weekends	Yes at weekends	Not generally available but contact prison probation officer	Visits are usually longer on Saturday afternoons and Sundays

Type of Prison	Category	Visiting Times	Public Transport	Special Transport
P **CAMP HILL** Clissold Rd Newport Isle of Wight PO30 5PB 0983-527661		1.45–3.45 pm daily	From Ryde bus 1, 1A from Ryde Esplanade. From Cowes bus 1, 1A from Carvel Lane to St Mary's Hsp, or hydrobus from Cowes which runs from hydrofoil terminal. Passengers should ask for Camp Hill	Abba coaches from London every Sun, tel. 01-403 5272. Adults £12.50, child 5–14 years £5.70 (inclusive of ferry fares). Seats *must* be booked in advance
YOI **CAMPSFIELD** **HOUSE** Langford Lane Kidlington Oxford OX5 1RE 086-75-4113	Closed Young Offenders and Remand Centre	1.30–3.30 pm daily	Bus no 2 from Oxford (Cornmarket) to Kidlington. Get off at 'The Moors' & follow airport signs	None
P 46 Longport **CANTERBURY** Kent CT1 1PJ 0227-762244	B Local	1.30–3.30 pm, Mon to Sat	Trains from London to Canterbury East or Canterbury West	None
P Knox Rd **CARDIFF** CF2 1UG 0222-491212	C Local Young Offenders Remand	Mon to Sat 1.30–3.30 pm. Privilege visits Mon to Fri only 1.30–3.30 pm	Train to Cardiff General, then bus to Dumfries Place or Blind Institute (20–25 mins walk from train station)	None
YOI **CASTINGTON** Morpeth Northumberland NE65 9XG 0670-760942	Young Offenders (long term)	1.30–4.30 pm daily	Train to Newcastle on Tyne. Metro to Haymarket. Bus 418 or X18 at 45 mins past hour. Takes 70 mins	From Cleveland. Leeds, S. Yorks and Cumbria, Manchester and Liverpool. Book via probation

Visitors' Centre	Canteen	Kids' Play Area	Overnight Stay	Notes
No	Drinks machine only	No	Overnight stay centre at Crocker St Newport. phone 0983–527970	No disabled facilities but only one very large step to negotiate – help can be obtained
No	Yes on Saturday	No	Plenty of B&Bs in Oxford	Visiting orders required for all visits except for unconvicted prisoners. Disabled access to ground floor visiting room easy
No	No	No	None	Privilege visiting orders cannot be used on Sats
No	Yes	Yes (but no toys)		Wheelchair access and disabled toilet
No	Yes	Yes	Contact prison probation	Full three-hour visit usually available. WRVS run sandwich and flask-filling service for return journey

Type of Prison	Category	Visiting Times	Public Transport	Special Transport
YOI CHANNINGS WOOD Denbury Newton Abbott Devon TQ12 6DW 0803-812361	C	Tue, Wed and Sat 1.30–3.30 pm	Train to Newton Abbot, Bus 120, 121 177, 178, 179, 195 to bus station. Bus to Denbury (very infrequent) alighting ½ mile from Denbury, or taxi from Newton Abbott costs about £6 return fare	Bus from Cardiff monthly. Book on 0222-32999. Bus from Hampshire probation: book on 0705-376554
YOI CHELMSFORD Essex CM2 6LQ 0245-268651	Young Offenders Local Remand	Tues and Thur 2.00–3.30 pm; Sat and Sun 1.15–3.00 pm	Trains from Liverpool St 35–40 mins. 20 min walk from Chelmsford Stn	None
P COLDINGLEY Shaftesbury Rd Bisley, Woking Surrey GU24 9EX 04867-6721	B	Remand prisoners: Mon–Fri 2.30–4.30 pm; Sat 9.30–11.30 am. Convicted prisoners: Sat 2–4 pm, Sun 10–12 am and 2–4 pm	Bus from Woking Station every 30 mins to Hen & Chickens	Coach from London Sunday afternoons. Contact Taylors Coaches, tel. 01-237 2707
P COOKHAM WOOD Rochester ME1 3LU 0634-814981	Closed Female	2–3.30 pm daily except Weds. 30 mins during week, possible 1 hr at weekends	Train, London Victoria to Chatham, then bus 162, 164, 166, but check at station	None

Visitors' Centre	Canteen	Kids' Play Area	Overnight Stay	Notes
No	Yes	No		Picnic area at prison. New 'Vulnerable' Prisoners' Unit' for long-term prisoners. Entrance at rear of prison. Own car park
No	Yes	No		At time of going to press Chelmsford was about to change its category, but no further details as yet
No	Yes Sat pm Sun am and pm	Yes Creche on Sat pm and Sun pm		Wheelchair access but no disabled toilets. Coldingley is an industrial prison so visits to convicted prisoners are normally at weekends
No	Yes at weekends	Yes	Contact prison probation	Ex-prisoners are not allowed to visit within three months of their release

Type of Prison	Category	Visiting Times	Public Transport	Special Transport
P **DARTMOOR** Princetown Yelverton Devon PL20 6RR 082-289-261	B	Tues to Fri 9.30–10.45 am, 2–3.30 pm. Weekends 9.30–10.45 am, 1.30–3.00 pm. Both sessions on one VO every four weeks, PVOs quarterly. No visits on Xmas Day, Boxing Day or Good Friday	Rail to Plymouth, taxi from Plymouth to Princetown. Tel. Princetown 224. About £6 each way	From Cardiff tel. 0222-32999 or Portsmouth 0705-376554
YOI **DEERBOLT** Bowes Rd Barnard Castle Co. Durham DL12 9BG 0833-37561	Closed Young Offenders	2–4 pm daily	Rail to Darlington. Hourly bus no 75 takes 50 minutes to Barnard Castle, then 15 minutes' walk	Coaches from Carlisle, Durham, Northumbria, Leeds. Book via probation
P 7 North Square **DORCHESTER** Dorset DT1 1JD 0305-66021	B Local	Remand prisoners: Mon to Fri 1.45–3.30 pm; Sat 1.30–3.00. Convicted prisoners: Mon to Fri 1.45–3.30 pm; Sun 1.30–3.00	10 minutes' walk from Dorchester railway station	Coaches run by Reading, Oxford, South Glamorgan, Gwent, West and Mid-Glamorgan and Hampshire Probation
YOI Western Heights **DOVER** Kent CT17 9DR CT17 9DR 0304-203848	Young Offenders	Sat and Sun 1.30–3.30 pm	Train from Charing Cross or Victoria. Walk or taxi from station – 1 mile uphill	None
P **DOWNVIEW** Hospital Road Sutton Surrey SM2 5PA 01-643 4338			Expected to open in July 1989	

Visitors' Centre	Canteen	Kids' Play Area	Overnight Stay	Notes
Yes. Non-resident visitors may use Wesley House facilities	Yes	No	Wesley House, Princetown. Tel. Princetown 365	On weekday afternoons, 1.45–4.45 children can be left at the Activity Group in the Family Centre where they will be supervised
No	Yes	Yes	None	No disabled access. Weather conditions can be severe so warm clothing is advised for the long walk from Barnard Castle in winter
Yes	No	No	Contact probation on 0305–69339 to arrange local B&B	
	Yes	No	Phone prison probation for details of local B&B	Easy access for wheelchairs

Type of Prison	Category	Visiting Times	Public Transport	Special Transport
YOI & YCC DRAKE HALL Eccleshall Staffs ST21 6LQ 0785-850621	Female Open	2-3.45 pm daily	Train to Stafford, then taxi (£12 return)	None
P Old Elvet **DURHAM** DH1 3HU 091-386 2621	B Local Female Closed	Remand prisoners: Mon to Sat 1.30-3.00 pm. Convicted prisoners: 1.30-3.30 pm daily	Train to Durham, then 20-minute walk	Coaches from Carlisle; tel. 0228-22333. Coaches from Doncaster, Barnsley, Sheffield, Rotherham and Liverpool; tel. 0709-64774 ext. 36
YOI & P EAST SUTTON PARK Sutton Valence Maidstone Kent ME17 3DF 0622-842711	Female Open	Sat and Sun, 1.45-3.45 pm. No visitors admitted after 3.15 pm	Bus/train to Maidstone. Bus 11, 12 or 59 to Sutton Valence, then 1½ mile walk	None
YOI EASTWOOD PARK Church Avenue Falfield Wotton under Edge Gloucestershire GL12 8DB 0454-260771	Closed Junior DC	Sat and Sun, 1.30-3.30 pm. After reception visit, once a fortnight unless parents separated, then with Governor's agreement one visit per week for each parent	Bus X20 and X21 from Bristol and Gloucester. Stop by church at Falfield	None
YOI & P ERLESTOKE HOUSE Erlestoke Nr Devizes Wiltshire SN10 5TU 038-081 3475	YOI	Professional visits: Mon to Fri 9.15-11.15 am. Domestic visits: 2-4.15 pm daily	BR to Westbury, then taxi	Monthly coach Cardiff Probation

Visitors' Centre	Canteen	Kids' Play Area	Overnight Stay	Notes
No	Yes	No		Easy access for wheelchairs. Baby-changing facilities
Yes, in Old Elvet	Yes No refreshments in remand visits area	Yes	Phone prison probation to get details of B&B	Disabled access. Last visits at 3.00 pm
No	Yes	No	No	Wheelchair ramps
No		No	Local hotels. Details from prison probation	No smoking
No	No	No	Contact prison probation to arrange B&B	There are fortnightly privilege visits

Type of Prison	Category	Visiting Times	Public Transport	Special Transport
YOI **EVERTHORPE** Brough N. Humberside HU15 1RB 04302-2471	Closed Young Offender Institution	1.30-3.30 pm daily	Limited bus service 155 Hull-Goole passes Brough station. For details phone 0482-27146	Probation service coach monthly from S. Yorks, W. Yorks, Cleveland, Northumbria
P New North Rd **EXETER** EX4 4EX 0392-78321	B Local	Mon to Sat 1.30-3.30 pm	Bus or train to Exeter and short walk	None
P New Rd **FEATHERSTONE** Wolverhampton WV10 7PU 0902-790991	C	1.40-4.30 pm daily. Privilege visits Mon to Fri only	Bus 872 Mon to Sat from Wolver-hampton bus station. Sunday service X90	Probation run coaches from Chesterfield, Nottingham and Leicester
YOI Bedfont Rd **FELTHAM** Middx TW13 4ND 01-890 0061	Young Offender and Remand Centre for young men under 21	Remand prisoners: Mon to Fri 1.30-3.30 pm; Sat only by prior arrangement 9.15-10.30 am. Convicted prisoners: Sat and Sun 1.45-3.30 pm	Trains Waterloo to Feltham. Bus 117 or 237 to Three Horseshoes, then 10-15 min walk	None
YOI **FINNAMORE** **WOOD** Frieth Rd Medmenham Marlow Bucks SL7 2HX 0494-881275	Open Young Offenders	Sat and Sun 1.30-3.30 pm	Sat and Sun: train from Marylebone to High` Wycombe, then taxi, plus Sat-only train from Paddington to Marlow, then taxi	None

Visitors' Centre	Canteen	Kids' Play Area	Overnight Stay	Notes
No	Yes Weekends	No		Visiting area on ground-floor level – disabled access easy
Yes	Yes	No	Contact prison probation	Visitors' centre on ground-floor level – special arrangements can be made for access
No	Yes	Yes		Privilege visiting orders can only be used at weekends in special circumstances. Phone prison to check
No	Yes			Fortnightly prison visits
No	Yes	No	None	No disabled facilities but staff will help disabled people over three steps into visits room. Finnamore Wood operates as part of Huntercombe YC

Type of Prison	Category	Visiting Times	Public Transport	Special Transport
P **FORD** Nr Arundel West Sussex BN18 0BX 0903-717261	D	1.30–3.30 daily. Privilege visits only Mon to Sat	Ford railway stn ½ mile from prison. Littlehampton 2–3 miles. Taxis available	None
P **FOSTON HALL** Foston Derby DE6 5DN 0283-78354	D	1.30–3.30 pm daily	Rail to Uttoxeter or Burton-on-Trent Hourly Stevensons bus from station to prison	Coach from Wolverhampton and Smethwick. Tel. 021–544 4636
P **FRANKLAND** Brasside Durham DH1 5YD 091–384 5544	B Dispersal	Mon to Fri 9.30–11.30 am, 2.00–3.45 pm; Sat and Sun 2.00–3.45 pm	Train/bus to Durham United bus no. 65, 20 minutes past hour	Special coaches: Nc Manchester, tel. 061–236 7621; S. Yorks, tel. 0709-364774/5/6; W. Yorks tel. 0532–43061; Merseyside, tel. 051–920 9201
P **FULL SUTTON** Moor Lane Full Sutton York YO4 1PS 0759-72447	B Dispersal	2.00–4.00 pm daily (Incl. weekends)	Train to York, then (weekdays) Inglebys coach from station to Full Sutton village. Departs at 12.28 pm. 10 mins walk to prison. Return bus leaves village at 4.35 pm. Weekends bus 744 from station 12.25 pm to Pocklington where prison minibus collects	None
P **GARTH** Ulnes Walton Lane Leyland Preston PR5 3NE 0772-621111	B	Opened 1989. No further details available at time of going to press		

Visitors' Centre	Canteen	Kids' Play Area	Overnight Stay	Notes
No	Yes	Yes	B&B available in Littlehampton	Disabled access
No	Yes	No	Contact prison probation for B&B information	Disabled access easy – visits room at ground level
	Yes	Yes	Contact prison probation for B&B information	
No	Yes	Yes	Contact prison probation for B&B (ext. 3028)	Baby-changing facilities. Ramp access to visiting area

Type of Prison	Category	Visiting Times	Public Transport	Special Transport
P **GARTREE** Leicester Rd Market Harborough Leicestershire LE16 7RP 0858-65041	B Dispersal	2.00–4.15 pm daily	Train to Market Harborough, then taxi £4. Prison bus meets train at weekends	Minibus from Wolverhampton alternate Wednesdays. Phone 0902-710621
YOI **GLEN PARVA** Tigers Road Saffron Rd Wigston Leicester LE8 2TN 0533-772022	B Youth Custody Centre	Remand prisoners: Mon to Fri 1.45–3.15 pm (last admission 2.45 am); Sat 9–11 am (last admission 10.30 pm). Convicted prisoners: Mon to Fri 1.45–3.15 pm (last admission 2.45 pm); Sat and Sun 1.30–3.15 pm	Train to Leicester, then Midland Fox bus 42 from St Margaret's bus station. Or train Leicester Sth to Wigston and 10 mins walk	
P Barrack Square **GLOUCESTER** GL1 2JN 0452-29551	B Local and Rule 43	YOI and convicted adult prisoners 1.30–3.30 pm daily excl. bank hols. Remand and civil prisoners Mon–Sat	Train/bus to Gloucester. 15 mins walk from station	None
P & YOI **GRENDON** Grendon Underwood Aylesbury Bucks HP18 0TL 0296-77301	B Psychiatric	Sat, Sun and Wed 1–3 pm	1225 bus (Red Rover) from Aylesbury. Only one bus connects with visits. No public transport on Sundays	Coach from W. Midland, tel. 021-233 4166 to book, plus coach service from London, Ace coaches, Southwark, tel. 01-837 4390 or 01-237 3894

Visitors' Centre	Canteen	Kids' Play Area	Overnight Stay	Notes
No	Yes	There is a space where children can run around	Contact Prison probation to arrange B&B	For disabled access contact prison prior to visit
No	Yes	No		No waiting room outside centre gates. Visitors for remand prisoners must arrive by 3 pm. Baby-changing facilities available. Disabled access good
No	Yes Refreshments except Thurs and bank hols	Yes – Mon, Tues, Wed and 2nd and 4th Sunday of month	No	Baby-changing room. Wheelchair access ramps
No	Yes	Yes	Contact prison probation office	Wheelchair access possible and quite easy. The bus from Aylesbury only runs on Sundays, April to October

Type of Prison	Category	Visiting Times	Public Transport	Special Transport
YOI **GUYS MARSH** Shaftesbury Dorset SP7 0AH 0747-53344	Open Young Offenders	Sat and Sun 1.30–3.30 pm. No entry after 3.15 pm	Train to Gillingham or bus to Shaftesbury. Minibus pick-up service from prison meets train at Gillingham at 1.05 pm	Coach from Hampshire: phone 0705–376554 to book
YOI Dolphin Way **HASLAR** Gosport Hants PO12 2AW 0705-580381	Young Offenders	Wed, Sat, Sun 1.30–3.00 pm	Rail to Fareham or Portsmouth Harbour. Bus to Gosport. No. 9 or 19 bus from Gosport ferry	None
YOI Thorne Road **HATFIELD** Doncaster S. Yorks DN7 6EL 0405-812336	Open Young Offenders	1–3.45 Sat and Sun only	Bus 187 from Doncaster via Hatfield village. Enquiries (S. Yorks Transport) tel. 0302–329666. Nearest BR main line: Doncaster Enqs. tel. 0302–340222	Newcastle/ Durham phone 091–284-2585. Also coaches from Leeds and Cumbria: contact probation to book
P **HAVERIGG** Millom Cumbria LA18 4NA 0657-2131	C	1.15–3.15 pm daily	Train to Millom. Bus 15 from Market Square	Leeds: tel. 0532-430601; Liverpool: tel. 051–920-9201; Manchester: tel. 061–236-7621; North East: tel. 091–266-7081; Carlisle contact probation
YOI **HEWELL** **GRANGE** Redditch Worcestershire B97 9QQ 0527-43843	Open Young Offenders	Sat and Sun only, 1.15–3.30 pm	Bus 147 Birmingham to Redditch every ½ hr. Bus 145 Birmingham to Bromsgrove hourly. Bus 318 Redditch to Bromsgrove passes side gate hourly	Coaches from Coventry, Birmingham, Wolverhampton. Book through probation

Visitors' Centre	Canteen	Kids' Play Area	Overnight Stay	Notes
No	Yes	No	List of addresses available from probation dept.	Wheelchair access quite easy
No	Yes	No		No smoking. Only three visitors at a time
No	Yes	No		No girlfriends under 18 allowed unless accompanied by parent. No more than three adults.
No	Yes	Yes	Contact prison probation to arrange B&B	Drinks vending machine takes 5p and 10p. Easy wheelchair access
No	Yes	Yes		Disabled access possible

Type of Prison	Category	Visiting Times	Public Transport	Special Transport
P **HIGHPOINT** Stradishall Newmarket Suffolk CB8 9YG 0440-820611	C and D	Weekend: 1.45–3.45 pm Midweek: privilege visits only	Bus 933 from Bury St Edmunds at 12.15 pm	Coach from Liverpool St station Tues, Thurs, Sat, Sun. Bookings 01-237 2707
YOI **HINDLEY** Wigan Lancs WN2 5TH 0942-866255	Closed Remand Centre Males under 21	1.30–3.30 pm daily	Train to Wigan, then bus 658 from bus station, Market St or Library St	
YOI **HOLLESLEY BAY** Hollesley Bay Colony Woodbridge Suffolk IP12 3JS 0394-411741	Open and Closed Young Offenders and DC	2.00–4.00 pm preferably at weekends	Ipswich, Woodbridge or Melton stations, No. 16 bus. Check with prison as it is infrequent	Coach every Sun from London, Chelmsford and Colchester, City Central Ltd. Enquiries and bookings 01-237 8076
P Parkhurst Rd **HOLLOWAY** London N7 ONU 01-607 6747	B Women's Prison	Mon to Fri 9.45–11.15 am, 1.30–3.30 pm; Sat, Sun 9.30–11 am, 1.30–3 pm. NO remand visits on Sunday	Underground to Caledonian Road. Buses 29, 253, 14 and 17 pass gate	None
P Hedon Rd **HULL** HU9 5LS 0482-20673	Local & YP Remand	Remand prisoners: Mon to Fri, 1.30–3.30 pm; Sat 1–3 pm. Convicted prisoners: Mon to Fri 1.30–3.30 pm; Sat 1–3, Sun 1.30–3.30 pm	Train to Hull, bus 78 or 76 from opp. station	Coach from Rotherham
YOI **HUNTERCOMBE** Huntercombe Place Nuffield Henley-on-Thames Oxon RG9 5SB 0491-641711/ 641715	Closed Young Offenders	Sat and Sun, 1.45–3.30 pm Weekday visits 30–45 mins by special arrangement only	Oxford coach from Victoria coach station, London stops 50 yards beyond entrance by Crown public house	None

Visitors' Centre	Canteen	Kids' Play Area	Overnight Stay	Notes
Café outside prison	Yes	No		Check before visit which side of the road the prisoner is on as there are two sides to this prison
No	Drink vending machine	No		
No	Yes	No		Check VO to find out which part of the prison the prisoner is in
No	No	No		No disabled access at present
Yes, at 13 Newtown Court opposite prison	Yes	No	Contact prison probation to arrange B&B	Good disabled access
No	Drinks dispenser at weekends	No	None	No smoking in visits room. Several steps into visits room. Severely disabled should notify staff before arrival

Type of Prison	Category	Visiting Times	Public Transport	Special Transport
P **KINGSTON** Milton Road Portsmouth Hants PO3 6AS 0705-829561	B Lifers	1.45–3.45 pm daily except Wed & Friday	Trains to Portsmouth and Southsea. Turn right out of station for 16a bus to St Mary's Hospital	
P **KIRKHAM** Preston PR4 2RA 0772-684343	D	Mon, Tues, Thurs and Sun 1.30–3.30 pm	Train to Kirkham from Preston, then taxi (£1) or bus from Preston to Kirkham Market Place and walk	Coaches from Humberside and W. Yorks. Book via probation
YOI **KIRKLEVINGTON GRANGE** Yarm Cleveland TS15 9PA 0642-781391	Young Offenders	1.30–3.30 pm daily	Rail to Eaglescliffe, then infrequent bus or taxi to Yarm	None
P The Castle **LANCASTER** LA1 1YL 0524-68871	C	Weekdays Tues & Thurs 9.30–11.15 am, 2.15–4.15 pm; Sat and Sun, 1.15–3.00 pm	Rail or bus to Lancaster	
RC **LATCHMERE HOUSE** Church Rd Ham Common Richmond Surrey TW10 5HH 01–948–0215	Remand C&D	Mon to Fri 1.30–3.30 pm; Sat 1.30–3.15 pm. Sat visits sometimes cancelled. Phone to check	Rail/tube to Richmond, 65 bus from Kingston Rd to Ham Common, then walk	None
P Armley **LEEDS** LS12 2TJ 0532-636411	B Local	Remand prisoners: Mon to Sat 12.30–3.15 pm Convicted prisoners: Mon to Sat 1.30–3.15 pm	Rail/bus to Leeds, Wellington St bus station, 40, 83, 72, 508 pass prison prison	

Visitors' Centre	Canteen	Kids' Play Area	Overnight Stay	Notes
No	Yes	Yes	Contact prison probation to arrange B&B	Contact prison in advance for dis- abled visitors – visiting room on ground-floor level
No	Yes	No	Local hotels. Contact prison probation	
No	Yes	No	Contact prison probation	Maximum three visitors. Travel information sent to parent/next of kin. No smoking. Visits room on ground level – easy access for wheelchairs
No	Yes	Crèche on Saturdays	Local B&B	Weekday visits at least 30 mins. Weekend visits 1 hr 45 mins
	Yes	No		Maximum three visitors. Unconvicted visits: 15 mins. minimum. Convicted visits: 30 mins. minimum.
Yes	Yes	Yes in visitors' centre	None	Remand prisoners are only allowed visits on alternate days

Type of Prison	Category	Visiting Times	Public Transport	Special Transport
P Welford Rd **LEICESTER** LE2 7AJ 0533-546911	B Local	Mon to Sat 1.30–3.30 pm	Rail/bus to Leicester, then 15-minute walk	
P Brighton Rd **LEWES** East Sussex BN7 1EA 0273-477331	Local	Convicted and remand prisoners: Mon to Fri 9.30–11.00 am, 1.30–3 pm; Sat and Sun 9.30–11 am	Rail/bus to Lewes	Minibus from Crawley, weekly. Tel. 0293-512450
P **LEYHILL** Wotton-under-Edge Glos GL12 8HL 0454-260681	D	1.30–4.00 pm daily	309 bus at 12.20 pm from Bristol toTortworth School	From Bristol Service 606 (Crown Coaches) every Tues. Dep 12.30 pm Bristol Temple Meads. Coach from Cardiff and Swansea: contact local probation
P **LINCOLN** Greetwell Rd Lincoln LN2 4BD 0522–533633	B Local	Remand prisoners: Mon to Fri 1.30–3.30 pm; Sat 9.45-11.15, 1.30–3.30 pm Convicted prisoners: Mon to Sat 1.30–3.30 pm, Sun 2–3.30 pm	Train to Lincoln central. Bus 5 to Queensway. Bus 18 or any county hospital bus to prison	
P **LINDHOLME** Bawtry Rd Hatfield Woodhouse Doncaster DN7 6DG 0302-846600	C&D	1.40–3.45 pm daily	Infrequent bus 186 from College Rd, Doncaster	Coaches from Manchester, Leeds and Newcastle: contact local probation service

Visitors' Centre	Canteen	Kids' Play Area	Overnight Stay	Notes
Yes	Yes but not Sats	Yes in visitors' centre		Contact prison to arrange disabled access. Visitors' centre tel. Leicester 544706. Open Mon to Fri 10.30 am–3.30 pm; Sat 12.30–3.30 pm.
Yes	Yes	Yes in visitors' centre	None organised	Disabled access not very good
No	Yes	Yes – outdoor play area	Family centre in Bristol. Book through probation	
Waiting room outside gate	Yes	No	Contact prison probation if necessary	No Sunday visits for unconvicted prisoners. WRVS shop in visits area. Wheechair ramps to visiting area.
Yes	Yes	Not available every day, only Mon, Fri and alternate weekends		Good disabled access

Type of Prison	Category	Visiting Times	Public Transport	Special Transport
P **LITTLEHEY** Perry Huntingdon CAMBS PE18 OSR 0480-812202	C	1.45–3.45 pm daily except Tues and Thurs	Train or bus to Huntingdon or St Neots, then 7 mile taxi journey – £7 each way	Coach from London. Coach service from Smethwick, Birmingham and Radmarket on alternate Thursdays and Saturdays. Phone 021-5444636 for details.
P 68 Hornby Rd **LIVERPOOL** L9 3DF 051-525-5971	B Local	1.45–3.00 pm daily	Train to Liverpool Lime St, then underground via Central to Rice Lane or Walton Junction	None
P **LONG LARTIN** South Littleton Evesham Worcs WR11 5TZ 0386-830101	B Dispersal	2–4 pm daily. Privilege visits Mon to Fri only	Evesham railway station. Prison van picks up visitors at 1.30 pm	None
YOI **LOWDHAM GRANGE** Nottingham NG14 7DA 0602-664451	Open Young Offenders	Sat and Sun 2–4.15 pm	Local train Nottingham Midland to Lowdham Station. Walk (2 miles) or taxi (tel. 633024 or 312152) or Barton's Bus No 7 from Victoria Centre to stop at Lowdham Grange Old Drive (½ mile walk)	None
RC **LOW NEWTON** Brasside Durham DH1 5SD 091-386-1141	B Remand Women and Young Men	1.30–3.30 pm daily	No 65 bus from bus station at Durham. Hourly service at 10 past hour	Coaches from Cumbria, S. Yorks, W. Yorks. Book through probation
P County Rd **MAIDSTONE** Kent ME14 1UZ 0622-55611	B	1.45–3.45 pm daily	5-minute walk from Maidstone East rail station (train from Victoria)	None

Visitors' Centre	Canteen	Kids' Play Area	Overnight Stay	Notes
Outside waiting room with facilities for changing and feeding babies	Yes	Yes – room off visits' area, supervised weekends only	No	Prisoners can have two visits per month but only one at weekends. Very bad for disabled access.
No	Yes	No	No	Provision for wheelchairs except on closed visits
Yes	Yes	Yes	The Woolpack, 12 Port St, Evesham, tel. 0386-47047, or book through probation	Some food can be taken to be eaten on visit. Check with the prison
No	Yes	No		No provision for wheelchairs but prison officers will facilitate access. If visitors are unable to visit at weekends they should contact House Management
No	Yes	No	B&B available through probation dept	Advance warning necessary for disabled visitors
No	Yes	Yes	Contact prison probation	Stairs to visits hall, but access can be arranged with advance warning

Type of Prison	Category	Visiting Times	Public Transport	Special Transport
P Southall St Strangeways **MANCHESTER** M60 9AH 061-834-8626	B Local	Remand prisoners: Mon to Sat 9.30–11 am, 1.30–3.15 pm Convicted prisoners: 1.30–3.15 pm daily	5-minute walk from Victoria station, 96 bus from Piccadilly station	None
P **MORTON HALL** Swinderby Lincoln LN6 9PS 0522-86245	D	Wed, Sat and Sun 2.15–4.00 pm	Train from Lincoln or Nottingham to Swinderby. 17 bus from Lincoln, 16 or 17 bus from Newark	None
YOI **THE MOUNT** Molyneaux Ave Bovingdon Hemel Hempstead Herts HP3 0NZ 0442-834363	Young Offenders	1.30–3.30 pm daily (except Wed, Good Fri, Christmas Day and Boxing Day) Sat 9.30–11 am	British Rail frequent services from London (Euston) to Hemel Hempstead. Bus from station to The Mount, London Transport, Metropolitan line to Chesham, bus from station to The Mount Green Line Coach Service 759 from London Victoria every Sunday to The Mount	None
P **NEW HALL** Dial Wood Flockton Wakefield W. Yorks WF4 4AX 0924-848307	Women's Remand Centre and Prison	Remand prisoners: Mon to Fri 1.30–3.30 pm; Sat 9.45–11.45 am. Convicted prisoners 1.30–3.30 pm daily	Train to Wakefield, Westgate or Huddersfield. Hourly bus (263) on the hour from Wakefield or from Huddersfield 231 (every 2 hours), then 1 mile walk from prison	None
YOI East Road **NORTHALLERTON** N. Yorks DL6 1NW 0609-780078	Closed Young Offenders	1.45–3.30 pm Tues and weekends	Train or bus to Northallerton, then walk	Coaches from Manchester or Sheffield probation

Visitors' Centre	Canteen	Kids' Play Area	Overnight Stay	Notes
Yes for remand prisoners' families	Refreshments in convicted visits area only	Crèche in convicted visits area only		Disabled access possible by prior arrangement
Yes	Yes	Yes – supervised crèche facilities	Guest house near prison. Contact prison probation	Visits centre on ground floor. Disabled access good. Up to three adults and children
No	Yes	No	No	Lift available for disabled visitors
No	Yes	No	B&Bs in Wakefield/ Huddersfield	Unconvicted visits 15 mins. Convicted visits 30 mins. Disabled access possible
No	No	No	Contact prison probation or casework officer for help in finding B&B	Vending machines available. No wheel-chair access available

Type of Prison	Category	Visiting Times	Public Transport	Special Transport
P NORTHEYE Barnhorn Road Bexhill-on-Sea East Sussex TN39 4QW 04243-5511	C	1.30–3.30 pm Wed, Thurs, Sat and Sun	Train to Bexhill, then 2-hourly bus 499 or taxi	None
P Mousehold **NORWICH** NR1 4LU 0603-37531	B&C	2–4 pm daily. See note re Sunday visits	Train or bus to Norwich, then bus 501, 502 or 509 to Vincent Road	None
P Perry Road Sherwood **NOTTINGHAM** NG5 3AG 0602-625022	B	1.30–3.45 pm weekdays, 1.30–3.30 pm weekends. Extra VO must be used on a weekday	Broad Marsh Centre (very near railway station) to Victoria Centre. Then buses 15, 16, 17, 18 or 19 from Trinity Sq. (opp Victoria Centre) to Perry Road	None
YOI ONLEY Rugby Warwickshire CV23 8AP 0788-52022	Closed Young Offenders	2.15–3.30 pm daily	Rugby rail station Mon to Sat Midland Red 582 departs 1.20 pm, returns 3.35 pm. No Sunday bus	Coach from W. Midlands and from Wolverhampton. Contact local probation
P New Road **OXFORD** OX1 1LX 0865-721261	B	Mon to Fri 1.45–3.30 pm; Sat and Sun 1.30–3.15 pm	Both central rail and bus stations are within a few mins. walk of the prison	
P PARKHURST Newport Isle of Wight PO30 5NX 0983-523855	B Dispersal	10.15–11.15 am, 2–4 pm daily. Both visits on one VO	Bus from Ryde Esplanade, 1, 1A towards Cowes, alight at Parkhurst or hydro bus from Cowes	From London – Abba coaches. Bookings/ enquiries 01-407 7013

Visitors' Centre	Canteen	Kids' Play Area	Overnight Stay	Notes
No	Yes	No	B&B in the area	Wheelchair access possible with help of prison officers.
Yes	Yes	Yes crèche, playbus and changing facilities	B&B locally. Contact prison probation	Main prison – Sunday visits for convicted and remand prisoners whose families live more than 50 miles away
No	Yes	Yes	Contact prison probation	Arrangements can be made for disabled people to visit in the welfare department. Contact probation in advance
Yes	No	Yes	Dunchurch or Rugby. Contact prison probation	
Yes. See notes	Yes	Yes	No	Disabled visitors can be accommodated if given prior notice. The Visitors' Centre is open from 1.30 pm on Weds and Thurs for refreshments and baby-changing room
No	Yes	No	Contact prison probation – local centre available	Visitors should expect to be searched. Easy access for wheel-chairs unless high risk visit.

Type of Prison	Category	Visiting Times	Public Transport	Special Transport
P **PENTONVILLE** Caledonian Rd London N7 8TT 01-609 1121	B Local	Remand prisoners: Mon to Fri and alternate Sats, 9.15–10.30 am, Convicted prisoners: Mon, Wed, Thurs, Fri, Sun 1.30–2.45 pm	Rail to King's Cross. Tube to Caledonian Rd. Buses 14, 45, 168a, 221, 259	None
YOI Easton **PORTLAND** Dorset DT5 1DL 0305-820301	Closed Young Offenders	Wed 2–3.45 pm; weekends 1.30–3.45 pm	Rail to Weymouth. Bus weekdays and Sat, 1B at 1.10 pm; Sunday bus 1	Coaches from Reading, Oxford West Glamorgan, Mid-Glamorgan, S. Glamorgan, Gwent, Avon, Plymouth, Portsmouth, Southampton
P 2 Ribbleton Lane **PRESTON** PR1 5AB 0772-57734	C and Remand	Remand prisoners: Mon to Fri 1.30–3.30 pm; Sat 1.30–3.15 pm. Convicted prisoners: 1.30–3.30 daily	Bus/rail to Preston, then walk ½ mile or bus from railway station to bus station, then walk ¼ mile	Coaches from Sheffield, Barnsley, Doncaster, Rotherham
RC **PUCKLECHURCH** Nr Bristol BS17 3QJ 0275-82-2606	B Women and Young Men	Mon to Sat 1.30–3.15 pm	Train/bus to Bristol/Temple Meads, then 388/389 bus to Pucklechurch	None
P **RANBY** Retford Notts DN22 8EU 0777-706721	C	Weekdays 2–4 pm; Sat and Sun 1.30–3.30 pm	Train to Sheffield and then Retford. Walk up Queen St to Babworth Road (5 mins) and catch any bus going to Worksop from opposite Catholic church	Coaches from Birmingham, Coventry, Leicester. Contact probation

Visitors' Centre	Canteen	Kids' Play Area	Overnight Stay	Notes
No	Yes	Yes	Contact Prisoners' Wives and Families Society, tel. 01-278 3981	No information on disabled access available. No convicted visits on Tues or Sat. No unconvicted visits on Sun
No	Yes	Yes	Contact prison probation	To book special transport phone local probation office. Stairs to family visits area but special arrangements can be made for disabled visitors
No	Yes (for convicted prisoners)	Yes (for convicted prisoners)		Wheelchair access to convicted visits only. No Sun visits for unconvicted prisoners. It's best to arrive early as visits close promptly
No	No	No	Bristol Family Centre, Gloucester Rd, Bristol. Tel. 0272-425994	Visits less crowded during week. Wheelchair access possible for females, difficult for males (3 flights of stairs)
No	Yes	Yes	Contact prison probation	You must take a VO or you will not be allowed to visit. Room to change a baby. Privilege VOs on weekdays only. Good access for disabled visitors

Type of Prison	Category	Visiting Times	Public Transport	Special Transport
P Forbury Rd **READING** Berkshire RG1 3HY 0734-587031	B Local	Remand prisoners: Mon to Sat 1.30–3.30 pm. Convicted prisoners: 1.30–3.30 pm daily	Bus or rail to Reading, then walk	
RC Warrington Rd **RISLEY** Warrington Cheshire WA3 6BP 0925-76 3871	B Women and Men	Remand males: Mon to Fri 1–3.30 pm; Sat 9–10.45 am. Convicted males: Sat 12.30–3 pm, Sun 1–3 pm. Remand females: Mon to Fri 12.30–3.30 pm; Sat 9–11 am. Convicted females: Sun 1–3.30 pm	Train to Warrington. Bus to Remand Centre	
YOI & RC ROCHESTER Kent ME1 3QS 0634-830300	Young Offenders/ Remand Adult/ Training	1.30–3.15 pm daily except Sundays	Train to Chatham or Rochester, then bus	None
P ROLLESTONE Rollestone Camp Shrewton Nr. Salisbury Wilts 0980-620 955	C	Weekends only	British Rail to Salisbury. Minibus available – enquiries through probation	Commercial coach from London. Contact Probation Office for details
P RUDGATE Wetherby W. Yorks LS23 7AZ 0937-844844	D	1.30–3.30 pm	From York bus to Tadcaster, then 78A bus, Leeds – bus 741. Wetherby bus 741	Coaches from Sheffield, Cleveland, Rotherham, Newcastle. Contact local probation
P SEND Woking Surrey GU23 7LJ 0483-223048	C	2–4 pm Tues, Wed, Sat, Sun	Train to Clandon, then 1½ mile walk. Train to Woking, then taxi (£12 return)	

Visitors' Centre	Canteen	Kids' Play Area	Overnight Stay	Notes
No	Yes	Toys available	Contact prison probation for list of B&Bs	Visitors with VOs can visit Sundays. Refreshments available daily
No	WRVS canteen available Saturdays only	Toys available in womens' visits area	Contact prison probation for list of B&Bs	Children under 16 can only visit a parent. People are often transferred quickly so check before visiting
No	Yes	No	Contact prison probation for details of B&B	Rochester has an uncertain future – possible change to adult prison at future date
No	WRVS canteen	No	Contact prison probation	Fortnightly privilege visits
No	Yes	Yes – supervised when busy		Babies feed bottles can be warmed. Disabled access possible with prison officer assistance
No	Yes	Yes	Contact prison probation for details of B&B	

Type of Prison	Category	Visiting Times	Public Transport	Special Transport
P Cornhill **SHEPTON MALLET** Somerset BA4 5LU 0749-3377	C	Domestic visits: Sun, Mon, Tues, Wed, Sat 1.30– 3.30 pm	Bus no. 376 from Bristol leaves at 11.15 am, Bristol to Wells, Badgerline bus from Wells to Shepton Mallet. Book straight through from Bristol	Coaches from Hampshire and Mid Glamorgan
P The Dana **SHREWSBURY** Salop SY1 2HR 0743-52511	B Local	Convicted and remand prisoners: Mon to Fri 9.30– 11.30 am, 1.30– 3.30 pm; Sat 9.30–11.30 am: Remand prisoners; Convicted prisoners 1.30– 3.30 pm	Train or bus to Shrewsbury, then short walk	
P **SPRING HILL** Grendon Underwood Aylesbury Bucks HP18 0TJ 0296-77301	D	1.00–3.00 Wed, Sat, Sun Also 9.00– 11.00 Sat & Sun. Wed, Sat and Sun 1–3pm. Also Sat and Sun 9–11 am	1225 bus (Red Rover) from Aylesbury bus station. No Sunday service in winter	Coach from W. Midlands – bookings 021-233-4166. Coach service from London every Sun – tel. 01-837 4390/ 237 3894 for booking enquiries
P 54 Goal Rd **STAFFORD** Staffordshire ST16 3AW 0785-54421	C	2–4 pm daily; Sat, Sun and Bank hols 1.30– 3.30 pm	Train to Stafford, then 10–15 minute walk	Coaches from Chesterfield, Nottingham, Derby, Luton, Bedford, Northampton, Leicester, Coventry, Birmingham and Wolverhampton

Visitors' Centre	Canteen	Kids' Play Area	Overnight Stay	Notes
No	Yes	Yes	Bristol Family Centre – tel. 0272-425994	The last bus in time for visits leaves Bristol at 11.15 am. In case of special difficulty – young children, etc. – contact prison probation in advance for help with transport
No	Yes	No	B&B can be arranged but is difficult in the summer tourist season	Visits end promptly at 3.30 pm. Visitors often have to wait a long time due to overcrowding. Check with prison before visiting prisoner as they are moved on very quickly. Wheelchair access and toilets
No	Yes	Yes	Contact prison probation officers on ext. 229 or 264	Wheelchair access is possible but not easy
Yes	Yes	No	Contact prison probation	Some restriction on the use of privilege visiting orders so check with prison

Type of Prison	Category	Visiting Times	Public Transport	Special Transport
P **STANDFORD HILL** Eastchurch Sheerness Kent ME12 4AA 079-588-441	D	Tues, Wed, Thurs, Sat and Sun, 1.30–3.30 pm	Train to Sheerness, then 362 bus to Eastchurch, then walk (20 mins)	Coach from London–contact Ace coaches on 01-237 3894 or 01-837 4390
P **STOCKEN** Stocken Hall Rd Stretton nr. Oakham Leics. LE15 7RD 0780-81771	C	Weds, Sat and Sun, 1.30–3.45 pm	Train to Stamford 10 miles, Oakham 11 miles, Grantham 14 miles, then taxi	Coach from Birmingham, Coventry, Chesterfield and Northampton. Contact probation
YOI **STOKE HEATH** Market Drayton Salop TF9 2JL 0630-4231	Closed Young Offenders	Weekday visits by arrangement; Sat and Sun 1.30–3.30 pm	Rail to Shrewsbury bus to Ternhill Crossroads, then walk 1 mile	Coach from Liverpool and Manchester. Contact probation. Sat special bus leaves Crewe Rail Station at 1pm, returning 1.45pm. Fare costs about £1.50
P & YOI **STYAL** Wilmslow Cheshire SK9 4HR 0625-532141	Closed Women's and Young Offenders	Wed and Sat 1.30–3.30 pm, up to 2hrs. Only ½ hour other days. No Sunday visits	Train to Manchester Piccadilly, then local train to Styal, then 10 min walk	None
P **SUDBURY** Derbyshire DE6 5HW 028378-511	D	1.30–3.30 pm daily. Privilege visiting orders valid weekdays only	Train to Burton-on-Trent, bus to Sudbury	Coach from Wolverhampton and Smethwick. Tel. 021-544 4636 to book
P **SWALESIDE** Brabazon Road Eastchurch Sheerness Kent ME12 4DZ 0795 88766	B	1.30–3.30 pm daily	Train to Sheerness, then 362 bus to Eastchurch, then 20 min walk	Coach from London–contact Ace coaches on 01-237 3894

Visitors' Centre	Canteen	Kids' Play Area	Overnight Stay	Notes
No	Yes	No	Contact home probation officer. B&B in Sheerness but difficult in summer	Use of privilege visiting orders Mon to Fri only
No	Yes	Yes	Enquire via home probation office. B&B in local towns.	Ramp for wheel-chairs at entrance. Visiting area on ground-floor level
No	Yes	No	B&B locally. Contact prison probation	No steps to visiting area; access by wheelchair quite good. Access to toilets, however, problematic due to narrow doorways
No	Yes Wed, Sat only	No	Very difficult to find accommodation locally	Prior arrangements necessary for wheelchair access
No	Yes	Yes		Baby-changing facilities available
No	Yes	Yes	Contact home probation officer. B&B in Sheerness but difficult in summer	No wheelchair access. Visits room on first floor

Type of Prison	Category	Visiting Times	Public Transport	Special Transport
P 200 Oyster-mouth Rd **SWANSEA** W. Glamorgan SA1 2SR 0792-464030	B Local	Mon to Sat 1.30–3.30 pm	Train to Swansea, bus to Quadrant bus station, then 5 minute walk	None
YOI **SWINFEN HALL** Lichfield Staffs WS14 9QS 0543-481229	Closed Youth Offenders	2–4 pm daily except Wed 2.45–4 pm	Bus or train to Lichfield or Trent Valley (or bus 901 from Birmingham passes door), then taxi. Prison minibus from station Sat 1.30 pm & 2 pm	None
YOI **THORN CROSS** Arley Rd Appleton Thorn Warrington Cheshire WA4 4RL 0925–602081	Open Young Offenders	Sat and Sun 1.15–3.45 pm	Rail to Warrington, bus 8 daily	None
P **THORP ARCH** Wetherby LS23 7AY 0937-844241	C	Tues and Thurs 2–4 pm; Sat and Sun 1.30–3.30 pm	Bus 741 from Leeds. Bus 78 from Harrogate	Coaches from various areas – check with probation office
YOI 29 Maryport St **USK** Gwent NP5 1XP 02913-2411	Young Offenders	Mon, Tue, Thurs, Fri and Sat 1.30–3.30 pm. Wed 2–3.30 pm. No Sunday visits	Rail to Newport, bus from Newport bus station at 12.15 pm	
USK YOI Prescoed Coed-y-Paen Pontypool Gwent NP4 0TB 02913-2231	Open Young Offenders	Sat and Sun 1.30–4.00 pm only unless by special arrangement	Rail to Newport, infrequent bus to Usk DC. Prison transport from the DC at 1pm, cost 50p	

Visitors' Centre	Canteen	Kids' Play Area	Overnight Stay	Notes
No	Yes	No	B&B in the area – contact prison probation	Wheelchair access possible with prison officer assistance
Sat and Sun 1–1.45 pm. Refreshments, etc.	Yes	Yes	B&B in Lichfield. Contact prison probation officer	Visits often last two hours
No	Yes at weekends	No		Good wheelchair access. Visits during the week may be restricted in duration
No	Yes	Yes	B&B locally. Contact prison probation office	Wheelchair access not very good
	Yes	No		
No	Yes	Yes		Baby-changing room available. Wheelchair access possible

Type of Prison	Category	Visiting Times	Public Transport	Special Transport
P **THE VERNE** Portland Dorset DT5 1EQ 0305-820124	C Training	Mon, Fri, Sat & Sun, 1.30– 3.30 pm. Privilege VOs Mon and Fri only	Rail to Weymouth, then service bus from Kings Statue, Weymouth to Victoria Sq, Portland. Taxi from Victoria Sq to prison	Coaches from Reading, Oxford, S. Glamorgan, Gwent, W. Glamorgan, Mid-Glamorgan, Hampshire. Contact probation
P Love Lane **WAKEFIELD** W. Yorks WF2 9AG 0924-378282	B Dispersal	Wed, Thurs, Sat and Sun, 1.30– 3.30 pm	Rail to Wakefield Westgate station, then walk	Coaches from Newcastle, Chester-le-Street Durham, Darlington, Manchester, Coventry. Contact probation
P **WANDSWORTH** Heathfield Rd Wandsworth London SW18 3HS 01-874 7292	B	1.30–3pm daily	Underground to Tooting Bec station, then walk along Trinity Rd; or train to Clapham Junction, then 77 or 19 bus; or train to Wands-worth Common	None
P **WAYLAND** Griston Thetford Norfolk IP25 6RL 0953-884103	C	1.50–3.50 pm daily. Privilege visits Mon to Fri only	Rail to Thetford or Attleborough, then taxi booked in advance on 0953-881388	Coach from London, tel. 01-237 2707 to book. Minibus from Chesterfield Contact probation
YOI Doddington Rd **WELLINGBOROUGH** Northants NN8 2NH 0933-224151	Closed Young Offenders	Tues, Thurs, Sat Sun, 1.45– 3.45 pm	Rail to Northampton. Bus 292, 293, 294, 295 to Wellingborough then bus 290 to second stop in Valley Rd	None
YOI **WERRINGTON** Stoke-on-Trent Staffs ST9 0DX 078130-3514	Closed Young Offenders	Wed, Sat, Sun 1.30–3.30 pm	Rail to Stoke-on-Trent. Bus 45, 47, 215–218 to Hanley, then bus to Werrington	None

Visitors' Centre	Canteen	Kids' Play Area	Overnight Stay	Notes
No	Yes	Yes	Phone Mr E.Mott on 0305-68794 for details of B&B	Arrangements for wheelchair access should be made with prison 2 weeks in advance
No	Yes	Yes	Contact prison probation officer	Wheelchair access possible. No disabled toilet facilities
No	Yes	No	None	There is no outside waiting room. Disabled access is not good but arrangements can be made
No	Yes	Yes	Contact prison probation officer	Arrangements can be made for wheelchair access if advance warning is given to prison. Room available for feeding and changing babies
No	No	No		No easy disabled access. Prisoners can opt for two 2-hour visits per month during the week or one 2-hour visit each month at weekends
No	Yes	No	Contact prison probation or unit manager for details of B&B	Good access for wheelchairs. No under-18s unless accompanied by an adult

Type of Prison	Category	Visiting Times	Public Transport	Special Transport
YOI York Rd **WETHERBY** LS22 5ED 0937-65141	Closed Young Offenders	1.15–3.30 pm daily. Weekday visits 30 minutes only	Rail to Leeds. Bus 796, 797, 798, 799, from W. Yorks bus station to Wetherby	Coaches from various areas – check with probation office
YOI **WHATTON** Nottingham NG13 9FQ 0949-50511	Young Offenders	1.30–3.30 pm daily	Rail to Nottingham. Bus to Bingham no. 102, then bus 413 Bingham to Whatton or taxi from Bingham	None
P Romsey Rd **WINCHESTER** SO22 5DF 0962-54494	Local prison and Remand Centre	Mon to Sat 1.30–3.30 pm Privilege visiting order Mon to Fri only	Rail to Winchester then walk or bus 22, 24, 25 or 66	Minibus for relations in Hampshire. Phone 0705-376554 to book
P **WORMWOOD SCRUBS** PO Box 757 Du Cane Rd London W12 0AE 01-743 0311	B	Mon to Fri 9.30–11 am, 1.30–3.30 pm; Sat 9.15–10.45 am, 1.15–3.15 pm but check in advance with prison before visiting on Sat	Underground to East Acton or bus 72	None
P **WYMOTT** Ulnes Walton Lane Leyland Preston Lancashire PR5 3LW 0772-421461	C	1.30–3.30 pm daily	Rail to Leyland, then bus 110 from Queens Hotel to prison at 1.04 pm Mon to Sat	Coaches from S. Yorks, W. Yorks, Birkenhead. Book via probation

Visitors' Centre	Canteen	Kids' Play Area	Overnight Stay	Notes
No	Yes at weekends	No		½ hour visits during week, 2-hour visits at weekends. Reasonable wheel-chair access
No	Yes	No		No smoking. No wheelchair access
No	Yes	Yes	Very difficult but some cheap B&Bs in Southampton	There is a super-vised crèche in the visits area. Support and information available from HALOW (Help and Advice Line for Offenders' Wives) on Tues and Sat pm. Good access for wheelchairs
No	Yes	No		Wheelchairs can be accommodated but no special facilities
No	Yes	Yes	Contact prison probation for details of local B&Bs	Two flights of stairs to visiting room – please give prior warning if assistance is required. Baby-changing room available. Buses from the prison back to Leyland are very infrequent so check times when you get to the prison

Appendix
Spent sentences

Under the Rehabilitation of Offenders Act 1974 certain criminal convictions become 'spent' or forgotten after a 'rehabilitation period'. This refers to a length of time which starts from the time of conviction. The rehabilitation period varies according to the length and type of sentence. Once this rehabilitation period is over an ex-offender is not normally obliged to mention the conviction when applying for a job, obtaining insurance or if involved in criminal or civil proceedings.

How long is a rehabilitation period?

It is not the amount of time actually served in prison that counts, it is the original sentence. Sentences of two and a half years or more never become spent. Other sentences become spent after fixed periods dating from the time of conviction.

- For a prison sentence (immediate or suspended) or young offender sentence of more than six months and less than two and a half years, the period is 10 years for people aged 17 or over when convicted and five years for those under 17.
- For immediate or suspended adult prison sentences, or young offender sentences of six months or less, the period is seven years for those over 17 when convicted and three and a half years for those under 17.
- A fine or community service order becomes spent after five years for anyone over 17 when convicted and two and a half years if under 17.
- For an absolute discharge the period is six months for those

over 17 at the time of conviction and three months for those under 17.
- For young people under 21 who have been sentenced to youth custody the period is seven years, and it is three years for being sentenced to a detention centre.

With some sentences the rehabilitation period varies.

- For probation, supervision, care orders, conditional discharge or bind over, the period is one year or until the order expires, whichever is the longer.
- For attendance centre orders, the period is one year after the order expires.
- For hospital orders (with or without a restriction order), the period is either five years or two years after the order expires (whichever is the longer).

Further convictions

If a rehabilitation period is still running when the person commits a petty offence (that is, a summary offence that can only be tried by a magistrates court), the petty offence will not affect the rehabilitation period still running. The rehabilitation period for each offence will expire separately.

However, if the further offence is one that could be tried in a Crown Court, then neither conviction will become spent until the rehabilitation periods for both offences are over. If the second conviction leads to a prison sentence of two and a half years or more, neither conviction will ever become spent.

Disqualifications

The rehabilitation period might vary if a person is disqualified at the same time as receiving another penalty. For instance, if a motorist is banned from driving for seven years *and* fined (which takes five years to become spent), the rehabilitation period would be seven years and not five.

Endorsements

A driving licence will be endorsed for either 3 years or 10 years. The rehabilitation period lasts as long as the endorsement.

Working abroad

The Act only covers Great Britain. Other countries have their own rules about whom they will give visas and work permits to. Embassies or overseas employment agencies should be able to provide information about this.

Convictions abroad

If a person is convicted abroad, courts in Great Britain will decide what sentence would have been passed for the offence here and the rehabilitation period will correspond to that sentence.

Disclosure of previous convictions

Exceptions to the Act

In some situations, people will be expected to declare their convictions whether spent or not. The principal ones are:

- Admission to certain professions which have legal protection, including lawyers, doctors, dentists, accountants, nurses and chemists.
- Appointment to certain sensitive offices and jobs, including the police, prison officers, probation officers, traffic wardens, teachers and social workers.
- Admission to certain regulated occupations, including firearms dealers, casino operators, directors and managers of insurance companies and unit trusts, and nursing home proprietors.
- Appointment to jobs where national security may be at risk, such as certain posts in the civil service or defence contractors.
- Applications for certificates for firearms, shotguns or explosives.

Employment

When an ex-offender is filling in an application form for a job, or is asked at an interview if they have any previous convictions, they can answer 'no' if the convictions are spent, providing the job applied for is not exempt under the Act. A spent conviction is not proper grounds for not employing someone or for sacking them under the terms of the Act.

However, if applicants do not disclose unspent convictions, they may be sacked and even prosecuted if they are found out.

Insurance

If an ex-offender is asked on a proposal form whether he or she has any previous convictions, the answer can be 'no' provided the convictions are spent. This is still the case even if the conviction is relevant to the risk which the insurers will underwrite. For instance, spent motoring convictions will not be required on a proposal form for motor insurance.

Criminal proceedings

Previous convictions can be cited in criminal proceedings even if they have become spent. The Lord Chief Justice and the Home Office have, however, advised the Crown Courts and the magistrates' courts that spent convictions should not be mentioned, except in very special circumstances.

Civil proceedings

In civil proceedings, no one should be asked questions which might lead to the disclosure of spent convictions. If such questions do occur, they can be ignored.

However, this rule does *not* apply in civil proceedings relating to children (adoption, guardianship, wardship, marriage custody, care and control, schooling), or in court proceedings when the court is satisfied that justice cannot be done unless evidence of spent convictions is admitted. Anyone with spent convictions can give consent to evidence being given about this if they so wish.

If the civil proceedings involve a matter exempt from the Act, see above.

The rule on civil proceedings also applies to arbitration proceedings, disciplinary proceedings, proceedings before an administrative tribunal, a club committee which has powers to affect anyone's rights, privileges, obligations or liabilities.

Confidential information

The Act makes it an offence for anyone with access to criminal records to disclose spent convictions to a third party. Someone with spent convictions may also be able to sue for libel any person making allegations about spent convictions (providing they can prove that the allegation was made with malice).

Further Information

Useful addresses

General

Central Office of Information
Hercules Road
London SE1 7DU
  To obtain free leaflets on
  legal aid write to:
  Home Office Publications
  (A) at this address.

House of Commons
Westminster SW1A 0AA
Tel. 01–219 4452

Police Complaints Authority
10 Great George Street
London SW1P 3AE
Tel. 01–273 3000
  Investigates complaints
  about the police.

Release
169 Commercial Street
London E1 6BW
Tel. 01–603 8654
Helpline. 01–603 8654
  Criminal legal advice, drug
  counselling and referrals;
  24–hour legal helpline.

Samaritans
17 Uxbridge Road
Slough
Berks SL1 1SN
Tel. 0753–32713
  24–hour confidential and
  free service to the suicidal
  and despairing; 20,000
  volunteers in 177 branches
  throughout the British Isles.

Terrence Higgins Trust
52–54 Grays Inn Road
London WC1X 8JU
Tel. 01–831 0330
  Advice, counselling, support
  and financial help available
  to people who have been
  diagnosed as HIV. Also
  provide information on HIV
  and AIDS.

Childcare

Childline
Freepost 1111
London EC4B 4BB
Tel. 0800–1111 (free)
   Support and counselling for young people who have been physically and/or sexually abused. Also helps adult women.

Child Poverty Action Group
4th floor
1–5 Bath Street
London EC1V 9PY
Tel. 01–253 3406
   Campaign for a fairer benefit system. Individual cases taken up. Referrals through advice agencies.

Children's Legal Centre
20 Compton Terrace
London N1 2UN
Tel. 01–359 6251
   Advice service 2–5 pm for children and adults including ex-prisoners. Also work to protect children's rights.

Family Rights Group
6–9 Manor Gardens
Holloway Road
London N7 6LA
Tel. 01–263 4016/7923
Tel. advice service.
01–272 7308
   National advice agency for parents in care proceedings including men and women in prison.

Family Service Units
207 Old Marylebone Road
London NW1 5QP
Tel. 01–402 5175
   Help families with problems of debt, delinquency, ill health, etc. Run summer play schemes.

Justice for Children
35 Wellington Street
London WC2 7BN
Tel. 01–836 5917
   Advice and information service for parents, children, social workers and lawyers on matters relating to the law and children.

National Council for One-Parent Families
   See under Prisoners, their partners and families

Immigration

Immigration Prisoners' Welfare
Richmond CAB
The Vestry House
21 Paradise Road
Richmond TW9 154
Tel. 01–940 9156
   Regularly visit Immigration Act detainees at Latchmere House and advise on welfare aspects of their case.

Joint Council for the Welfare of Immigrants
115 Old Street
London EC1V 9JR
Tel. 01–251 8706
    JCWI offer help, information
    and advice to prisoners with
    problems with the
    immigration laws or who
    are threatened with
    deportation.

Refugee Arrivals Project
Room 2005
2nd floor
Queens Building
Heathrow Airport
Hounslow TW6 1DL
Tel. 01–759 5740/1
    Assist and advise persons
    claiming to be refugees on
    arrival in the UK.

Refugee Unit
2nd floor
County House
190 Gt Dover Street
London SE1 4YB
Tel. 01–357 7421
    Make applications for
    persons claiming refugee
    status.

United Kingdom Immigrants Advisory Service (UKIAS)
2nd floor
County House
190 Gt Dover Street
London SE1 4YB
Tel. 01–357 6917
    A government-funded
    advice agency set up to
    advise and represent people
    in immigration appeals.

Law Centres

Avon and Bristol
Law Centre
Bedminster Parade
Bristol BS8 4HL
0272–667 933

Adamsdown
Law Centre
15 Splott Road
Splott
Cardiff CF2 2BU
0222–498 117

Belfast Law Centre
7 University Road
Belfast BT7 1NA
0232–321 307

Battersea and Wandsworth
Law Centre
248 Lavender Hill
London SW11 1LJ
01–228 9462/2566

Bradford
Law Centre
31 Manor Row
Bradford BD1 4PX
0274–306 617

Brent Community
Law Centre
190 Willesden High Road
London NW10 2PB
01–451 1122

Brent Young People's
Law Centre
272 Willesden High Road
London NW10 2PB
01–451 2428

Brighton
Law Centre
36a Duke Street
Brighton BN1 1AG
0273-296 34

Brixton
Law Centre
506-508 Brixton Road
London SW9 8EN
01-733 4245

Camden Community
Law Centre
2a Prince of Wales Road
London NW5 3LG
01-485 6672

Castlemilk
Law Centre
30 Dougrie Drive
Glasgow G45 9AD
041-634 0313

Central London
Law Centre
c/o 18-19 Warren Street
London W1P 5DB
01-437 5854

Coventry Legal and Income
Rights Centre
The Bridge
Broadgate
Coventry CV1 1NG
0203-223051/3

Dudley Law Centre
96a High Street
Dudley DY1 1QP
0384-239 243

Ealing Law Centre
Steyne Hall
Rectory Road
London W3 9NR
01-993 7801

Gateshead Law Centre
Swinburne House
Swinburne Street
Gateshead
Tyne and Wear NE8 1AX
091-477 1109

Gloucester Law Centre
Widden Old School
Widden Street
Gloucester GL1 4AQ
0452-423 492

Greenwich
Law Centre
187 Trafalger Road
London SE10 PTQ
01-853 2550

Hackney
Law Centre
236/238 Mare Street
London E8 1HE
01-986 8446

Hammersmith and Fulham
Law Centre
106/108 King Street
London W6 0QP
01-741 4021

Handsworth
Law Centre
220 Soho Road
Birmingham B21 9LR
021-554 0868/
551 1969

Harehills and Chapletown
Law Centre
263 Roundhay Road
Leeds LS8 4HS
0532–491 100

Highfield and Belgrave
Law Centre
Seymour House
6 Seymour Street
Highfields
Leicester LE2 0LB
0533–532 928

Hillingdon
Legal Resource Centre
12 Harold Avenue
Hayes
Middlesex UB3 4QW
01–561 9400/9440

Hounslow
Law Centre
51 Lampton Road
Hounslow
Middlesex
01–570 9505

Hyson Green
Law Centre
65 Birkin Avenue
Nottingham NG7 5AW
0602–787 813

North Islington
Law Centre
161 Hornsey Road
London N7 6DU
01–607 2461

South Islington
Law Centre
131/132 Upper Street
London N1 1QP
01–354 0133

North Kensington
Law Centre
74 Golborne Road
London W10 5PS
01–969 7473

Leicester
Rights Centre
6 Bishop Street
Leicester LE1 6AF
0533–553781

North Lambeth
Law Centre
381 Kennington Lane
London SE11 5QY
01–582 4425/4373

North Lewisham
Law Centre
28 Deptford High Street
London SE8 3NU
01–692 5355

Liverpool 8 Law Centre
34/36 Princes Road
Liverpool 8 1TH
051–709 7221/7222

North Manchester
Law Centre and
Community Services Centre
Paget Street
Manchester 10 7UX
061–205 5040

South Manchester
Law Centre
584 Stockport Road
Manchester 13 0RQ
061–225 5111

Middlesbrough
Law Centre
St Mary's Centre
82/90 Corporation Road
Cleveland TS1 2RW
0642–223 813/7

Newcastle Law Centre
85 Adelaide Terrace
Newcastle Upon Tyne
NE4 8BB
091–273 1210

Newham Rights Centre
285 Romford Road
London E7 9HJ
01–555 3331

Paddington Law Centre
439 Harrow Road
London W10 4RE
01–960 3155

Plumstead
Law Centre
105 Plumstead High Street
London SE18 1SB
01–855 9817

Roehampton and
Putney Law Centre
162 Upper Richmond Road
London SW15 2SL
01–789 8232

Salford Law Centre
498 Liverpool Street
Salford M6 5QZ
061–736 3116

Saltley Action Centre
2 Alum Rock Road
Birmingham B8 1JB
012–328 2307

Sheffield Law Centre
1st floor
Yorkshire House
Leopold Street
Sheffield S1 2GZ
0742–731 888

Southall
Community Law Centre
11B King Street
Southall
Middlesex UB2 4DF
01–574 2434

Southwark Law Centre
29 Lordship Lane
London SE22 8EW
01–299 1024

Springfield
Legal Advice Project
Springfield Hospital
6 Glenburnie Road
London SW17 7DJ
01–767 6884

Stockton Law Centre
Old Town Hall
Mandale Road
Thornaby
Cleveland TS17 6AW
0642–605 060

Stockwell and Clapham
Law Centre
337 Wandsworth Road
London SW8 2JT
01–720 6231

Thamesdown Law Centre
26 Victoria Road
Swindon
Wiltshire SN1 3AW
0793–486 926/7

Tooting and Balham
Law Centre
107 Trinity Road
London SW17 7SQ
01-672 8749

Tottenham Law Centre
15 West Green Road
London N15 5BX
01-802 0911

Tower Hamlets Law Centre
341 Commercial Road
London E1 2PS
01-791 0741

Warrington Law Centre
64/66 Bewsey Street
Warrington WA2 7JQ
Cheshire
0925-51104

West Hampstead Law Centre
59 Kingsgate Road
London NW6 4TD
01-328 4501/4523

Wolverhampton Law Centre
2/3 Bell Street
Wolverhampton WV1 3PR
0902-771 122

Wythenshawe Law Centre
Fenside Road
Sharston
Manchester M22 4WZ
061-428 5929

Prisoners, their partners and families

African–Caribbean Prisoners Support Group
35-37 Electric Avenue
London SW9 8JP
Tel. 01-326 4186
> Offer a social welfare service
> for black people in prison
> and on release. They are
> also involved in campaigning.

African Womens' Association
135 Clarence Road
Hackney
London E5 8EE
Tel. 01-985 0147
> Advice, information and
> support group for African
> women.

APEX Trust
Brixton Hill Place
London SW2 1HJ
Tel. 01-671 7633
> Help for ex-prisoners trying
> to get work. Provide skills
> training, guidance and
> counselling at various
> centres nationally.

Asian Women in Prison Group
134 Minet Avenue
Harlesden
London NW10 8AP
Tel. 01-961 5701
> Practical help with warm
> clothing and emotional
> support for Asian women in
> prison. They also campaign
> about prison conditions and
> the treatment of Asian
> women in prison.

Assisted Prison Visits Unit
11th floor
Calthorpe House
Hagley Road
Birmingham B16 8QR
Tel. 021–455 9855
    Provides payment for
    families on low income
    visiting prisoners on
    remand or convicted.

**Black Female Prisoners'
Scheme**
Brixton Enterprise Centre
444 Brixton Road
London SW9 8EJ
Tel. 01–733 5520
    Advice and help for black
    women in prison and after
    release. Information about
    housing, deportation,
    benefits, etc.

**Creative and Supportive Trust
(CAST)**
Basement
34a Stratford Villas
London NW1 9SG
Tel. 01–485 0367
    Group of women ex-prison-
    ers. Run drop-in centre for
    information, support and
    cups of tea, and creative
    training workshop. Can
    meet people at the gate on
    release and give support.

**Catholic Social Service for
Prisoners**
189a Old Brompton Road
London SW5 0AR
Tel. 01–370 0883
    Practical help to prisoners,
    ex-prisoners and their
    families, of any religion or
    none. Groups of CSSP
    volunteers operate in
    Preston, Durham and
    London as well as other
    areas.

First Generation
77 Atlantic Road
Brixton
London SW9 8PU
Tel. 01–733 0077
    Cater mainly for black
    people in South London.
    Advice and support offered
    from the point of arrest.
    Volunteers will visit prisoners
    and support families. After
    release they provide back-
    up facilities through the
    community centre.

Gingerbread
35 Wellington Seet
London EC2E 7BN
Tel. 01–240 0953
    Self-help organisation for
    one-parent families in
    England and Wales. Many
    local self-help groups.

Help and Advice Line for Offenders' Wives (HALOW)
Head Office
5 Onslow Road
Southampton SO2 0JD
Tel. 0703–229359

1 Printing House Street
Birmingham B4 6DF
Tel. 021–236 8931

30 Blackford Street
Winson Green
Birmingham B18 4BN
Tel. 021–523 4898

Liverpool
Tel. 051–548 6102

> Give advice and practical support to relatives of men in prison. Run a 24–hour crisis line from Southampton office.

Howard League for Penal Reform
320–322 Kennington Park Road
London SE11 4PP
Tel. 01–735 3317

> Campaigning organisation. Can answer queries from prisoners and families but do not provide legal advice.

Inner London Probation Service
After-Care and Resettlement Group
289 Borough High Street
London SE1 1JG
Tel. 01–407 4611

> Work with ex-offenders who are homeless and rootless and have no real ties with any particular area or probation officer. If you want to be referred to them speak to the prison probation department.

Inquest
Ground floor
Alexandra National House
330 Seven Sisters Road
Finsbury Park
London N4 2JP
Tel. 01–802 7430

> Campaign in the area of deaths in custody. Also will help families or friends get full and open inquiries.

Irish Commission for Prisoners Overseas
c/o 15 St John's Villas
Upper Holloway
London N19 3EE
Tel. 01–263 1477

> Help and information for Irish-born prisoners and their families.

Jewish Welfare Board
315/317 Ballard's Lane
London N12 8LP
Tel. 01–446 1499

> Offer social work support and assist Jewish prisoners in need. Write in.

Justice
95a Chancery Lane
London WC2A 1DT
Tel. 01–405 6018
Campaign for law reform.
Can help prisoners by
investigating where there is
a valid complaint about
conviction or sentence.
Emphasis mainly on longer
sentence prisoners.

Latin American Women's Service
Priory House
Kingsgate Place
London NW6 4TA
Tel. 01–372 6408
Advice, information and
support for Latin American
women.

National Association for the Care and Resettlement of Offenders (NACRO)
169 Clapham Road
London SW9 0PU
Tel.01–582 6500
Provide housing,
employment education/
training and re-settlement
services for ex-offenders
and others. Provide
information on penal affairs
and for prisoners' families.

NACRO Education Advisory Service
2 Hulme Street
Off Oxford Road
Manchester M1 5QA
Tel. 061–236 2604
Advice on education and
training nationally for
ex-offenders.

National Council for Civil Liberties
21 Tabard Street
London SE1 4LA
Tel. 01–403 3888
Legal advice on all aspects
of the criminal justice
system including treatment
in prison.

National Council for One-Parent Families
255 Kentish Town Road
London NW5 2LX
Tel. 01–267 1361
Free and confidential advice
and information service for
all one-parent families and
single pregnant women.
May take up individual
cases.

New Bridge
1 Thorpe Close
Ladbroke Grove
London W10 5XL
Tel. 01–969 9133
Befriending service for
prisoners during sentence
and after release. Job-finding
and job advisory service
operates from London and
Alton in Hampshire.

Northern Ireland Association for the Care and Resettlement of Offenders (NIACRO)
22 Adelaide Street
Belfast BT2 8GD
Tel. 0232–320157
Provide information,
transportation, practical and
emotional support for
prisoners' families.

PAIN
BM–PAIN
London WC1N 3XX
Tel. 01–542 3744
  An umbrella organisation
  incorporating PROP,
  Women in Prison, Radical
  Alternatives to Prison,
  INQUEST and the Black
  Female Prisoners' Scheme.
  If you are not sure which of
  these organisations would
  be most helpful, then write
  to PAIN who will pass your
  letter to whichever is the
  most suitable.

**Partners of Prisoners and
Family Support Group
(POPS)**
Room 278
Corn Exchange
Corporation Street
Manchester M4 3BP
Tel. 061–835 2442
  Friendship and advice to
  families and friends of
  prisoners. Self-help support
  groups in Manchester.
  Although Manchester based
  they are willing to help
  anyone from the North of
  England or North Wales.

Police Holding Unit
New Scotland Yard
Tel. 01–603 8654
  Can tell you over the
  telephone which prison
  recently-admitted prisoners
  have been sent to but you
  may have to hang on for
  quite a long time.

**Prisoners' Families Information
Centre**
Winsley's House
High Street
Colchester
Essex CO1 1UG
Tel. 0206–571457
  Give information and advice
  on practical problems and
  emotional support to
  families of prisoners in the
  Colchester area.

Prisoners' Location Index
c/o HMP Cleeland House
Page Street
London SW1P 4LN
  Can put you in touch with
  prisoners, but not those
  recently admitted. Write
  only.

Prison Reform Trust
59 Caledonian Road
London N1 9BU
Tel. 01–278 9815
  Campaign for better
  conditions in prison and the
  greater use of alternatives to
  custody. Can deal with
  enquiries on aspects of
  imprisonment and
  complaints about the
  treatment of individuals in
  prison, but no facilities to
  deal with cases of wrongful
  conviction. Provide free
  information pack for
  prisoners.

PROP
BM–PROP
London WC1N 3XX
Tel. 01–542 3744

An ex-prisoner organisation which handles enquiries from prisoners and their families from an ex-prisoner stand-point. Can provide legal and medical back-up in cases of complaints about prison treatment.

Prisoners' Wives and Families Society
254 Caledonian Road
London N1 0NG
Tel. 01–278 3981

Self-help group for prisoners' families. Offer information/ advice. Overnight stay hostel for families visiting London prisons or passing through on the way to a visit. Can offer holidays to prisoners' families.

Prisoners' Wives Service
51 Borough High Street
London SE1 1NB
Tel. 01–403 4091

Advice and information service for relatives or friends of prisoners in the Inner London area only. Can also visit prisoners' families and offer advice and friendship.

Rastafarian Advisory Centre
17a Netherwood Road
London W14 0BL
Tel. 01–602 3767

Befriending service for Rastafarian and other black prisoners. Arrange visits to prisoners. Give support to families, plus help and advice on release.

Rehabilitation and After-Care Project
15 Oldridge Road
London SW12 8PO
Tel. 01–673 0595

Cater particularly for the needs of black offenders and their families. Visit prisoners, maintain links between young offenders and their families. Provide legal help.

SACRO (Scottish Association for the Care and Resettlement of Offenders)
220 Renfrew Street
Glasgow G3 6TX
Tel. 041-332 176

Provides help, advice and a home visiting service for prisoners' families in Strathclyde through its Family Services Section.

Women in Prison
25 Horsell Road
London N5 1XL
Tel: 01-609 7463
An organisation for ex-prisoners that campaigns on aspects of womens' imprisonment. Contact from women prisoners about any aspect of imprisonment is welcomed.

Women Prisoners' Resource Centre
Room 1
1 Thorpe Close
Ladbroke Grove
London W10 5XL
Tel: 01-968 3121
WPRC workers regularly visit all women's prisons to give advice and information about housing and other facilities open to women returning to the London area. Provides advice and support for women after release. Free information pack for prisoners.

Useful Publications

Publications used in preparing this book

Mama, Amina, Mars, Maria and Stevenson, Prue. *Breaking the Silence: Women's Imprisonment*, available from the Women's Equality Group, London Strategic Policy Unit, Room 401, Middlesex House, 20 Vauxhall Bridge Road, London SW1V 2SB, tel. 01–633 1113.

National Association for the Care and Resettlement of Offenders. *NACRO Briefing Papers*, produced regularly by NACRO, many dealing with aspects of the prison system; *Children*, produced by the Prison's Link Unit. Both are available from NACRO, 169 Clapham High Road, London SW9 0PU, tel. 01–582 6500.

National Association of Probation Officers. *NAPO Probation Directory*, published annually in January. The directory contains the names of every probation officer in the UK working outside the prisons, listed under their area office, together with addresses and telephone numbers, as well as those of prison department establishments and other related miscellaneous addresses. Available from Owen Wells (publisher), 23 Eaton Road, Ilkley, West Yorks LS29 9PU, tel. 0943–602270.

Plotnikoff, Joyce. *Prison Rules: Working Guide* (1988), available from the Prison Reform Trust, 59 Caledonian Road, London N1 9BU, tel. 01–278 9815.

Prison Reform Trust. 'Prisoners' Information Pack' (1989). Available from the Prison Reform Trust at the above address.

Women Prisoners' Resource Centre. 'Reception Pack' (1988), available from Women Prisoners' Resource Centre, 1. Thorpe Close, Ladbroke Gove, London W10 5XL, tel. 01–968 3121.

Other useful publications

National Association for the Care and Resettlement of Offenders. *Outside Help* (1989), gives practical information for prisoners' families, dependants and friends. Updated regularly and available from NACRO, 169 Clapham Road, London SW9 0PU, tel. 01–582 6500.

If you want to receive regular updated information on any aspect of the criminal justice system you would be well advised to become a regular subscriber to NACRO. You can do this in three ways:

- by subscribing to *NACRO Briefings'* mailings, to receive six mailings a year of briefing papers and report summaries plus a twice-yearly publications list
- by subscribing to *NACRO News Digest*, to receive a twice-monthly round-up of key events, reports, statistics, speeches, parliamentary answers and legislation relating to the criminal justice system plus a publications list
- by becoming a member of NACRO and receiving six mailings a year of *NACRO Briefings*, report summaries and the NACRO *News Digest*, plus an annual report and publications list

Contact the Information Department, NACRO.

The Prison Reform Trust does not have a formal membership list but you can join a subscription scheme for one year to receive all the trust's reports and publications for one year. You can also keep in touch with current issues in penal policy by subscribing to the quarterly magazine *Prison Report*. Topics covered in recent issues include: privatisation, electronic tagging, AIDS, boards of visitors, parole and the future of probation.

If you do not wish to join a subscription scheme send for an up-to-date list of books and pamphlets, Juvenile Justice Project papers, general reports and papers. The trust's current publications include 'A Look Inside', a resource pack about prisons and alternatives to custody, and the 'Prisoners' Information Pack'. Contact the Prison Reform Trust, 59 Caledonian Road, London N1 9BU, tel. 01–278 9815..

Index